Hymns for the Gods

HYMNS

FOR THE

GODS

From Olympus to Asgard

Prayers in the Orphic and Eddic Traditions

PUBLISHED
by
HELIOTROPH BOOKS

@Heliotrophy on Twitter
heliotropospress@gmail.com
www.heliotroph.org

Our aim is to tackle postmodern malaise through the discussion and promotion of polytheism, Platonism, health and physical culture, and wealth/community building.

COVER ILLUSTRATION
by
BRENDAN HEARD
of the
AUREUS PRESS

@Trad_West_Art on Twitter
@AureusPress on Facebook
www.aureus-press.com

CONTENTS

Introduction

Hymns

Welcome

The book which you are now holding in your hands is, first and foremost, an act of devotion by someone whose life has been touched in the most profound and intimate ways possible by the forces to whom this work is dedicated. The peculiar sequence of circumstances that led here has at times seemed random, at other times seemed fated, and at many points been quite funny. The strange combination of rabbit holes that leads a person in the modern world not only to genuine religiosity but also to the conviction that the practices of our most ancient predecessors are wholly legitimate and powerful must surely be an entertaining one.

Seemingly absurd on its face, the apparent obstacles melt further and further away the closer one draws. The human animal has not been too severely altered since those days, so why should his ability to access their wisdom be? More importantly, his eternal soul has not changed either.

The modern Westerner is born into a world where even in spaces that do not attack or mock religiosity, faith is essentially extraneous, frivolous. There is little or no social pressure to devote serious effort to spiritual matters, and social pressure is one of the primary drivers of behavior. The result is that many people are left to either tend to their religious needs alone or to drift further and further away from the mainstream in search of community.

The latter outcome is probably quite beneficial in this age as the center hollows out and crumbles, but as for the former, the dangers of excessively individualistic practice should be obvious. Sadly this line of thinking may be anathema to many neopagans who cherish their eclecticism, as well as to people who are new to spirituality and carry with them the residue of atomized society. An overly individual practice will often leave the practitioner having to choose between being openly devout but isolated or else to be so private and camouflaged into the mainstream that their spiritual life suffers and may even atrophy. This is where so many people with serious spiritual potential get stuck. The residual prevalence of Abrahamist institutions and cultural references make them the easy choice, so few people are exposed to serious polytheism in the first place to know it's an option. Realistically, for people without the time or resources to invest in serious study, it just isn't an option at all yet - thus our creation of this book. Contrast this to organized faiths which have a simple and specific script for all laypeople, and the fact that we have any presence at all is a testament to how compelling and common-sense our case is.

Our argument at its simplest can be stated as such: The cultures to which our pre-dark age ancestors belonged, incredibly vibrant and sophisticated cultures at that, possessed a valid way of approaching the divine and incorporating it into their lives. A higher-definition statement of our argument would add that the disenchanted and atomised condition of the modern world, paired with the sclerosis and inflexibility of existing Abrahamic traditions, is crying out not for the prescriptive solutions of techno-pharmaceutical transhumanism but for the radical re-divinization of the entire world from the smallest blade of grass to the widest ocean, a return to a world full of Gods where every thought and action is not a switch being flipped but a prayer rolling through clear water.

We affirm that the mystic and perennial truths elucidated by the Orphic, Platonist, Asatru, and Vedic traditions are in fact uniquely and providentially suited to addressing the problems of modernity and post-modernity because they teach us the proper relationship of our selves to our experience, our selves to others, our selves to our spaces, and our selves to their source and cause. They lift our eyes upwards to reveal the fantastic and mysterious motions of the web of forces above us and give us the opportunity to live our lives attuned to that divine clockwork instead of being mindlessly tossed about by it.

They teach us to understand the world as not as an isolated creation of the divine but as a part of it, a reflection of it, a thing which is divine itself and so carries and reflects the divine hierarchy within it. There is much more to the cosmos than the material, there are layers and layers of spirits and Gods above the plane we find ourselves on, but none of these layers were ever understood to contradict or conflict with what we experience materially. And so in a pagan worldview the advancement of scientific understanding and of technology does not shake or threaten the foundations of our beliefs and practices, while at the same time we are spared the childish hubris of having to use empiricist consequentialism to jury-rig meaning out of the corpse of a dead world.

We are taught that there is an ineffable, impossibly subtle, impossibly magnificent First Principle, a principle of oneness and goodness that unites even being and non-being, a One which "neither Is nor is One." It lacks all things and abounds in all things, and we do not call it God because it has no differentiation by which it could be conscious or unconscious, godly or ungodly. Instead its impossible superabundance is refined into conscious, intelligible, intellectual, spiritual, and material realities by the Gods who, possessing noetic vision, unfold themselves from it to produce Being and then unfold all subsequent things from themselves, aiming to imitate and adore the Good in its superabundance.

As the Gods pour out their Being into increasingly particularised, individuated sets of Forms and minds, they create the declining planes of existence which "asymptotically" approach nothingness. That is to say that being descends closer and closer to the non-being of the One without ever fully arriving there. Thus matter is actually formed by a divine fire's nearness to emptiness, and its distance from the Being of the One is simultaneously its nearness to the non-being of the One; Hestia is first and last, youngest and oldest.

In practical terms, here on Earth we are incarnated into the "plane beneath the Moon," the point at which souls drift close enough to nothingness to mingle with matter and proceed to animate bodies. Our goal from this point, if we are well ordered and properly compelled towards the Good, is to return our conscious experience to our origins in the Gods and ultimately the One. This is not the destruction or rejection of our bodies, simply the recovery of a sense of selfhood and "I-ness" that is nestled in the absolute instead of the contingent. It is not the destruction and dulling of our senses; even the Gods witness all that happens here, but they are held aloof from suffering by the total self-knowledge that they are prior and superior to matter just as we are prior and superior to the hairs on our leg or the calluses on our feet. It is their knowledge that we seek to re-assimilate ourselves to.

This is not gnosticism; the world is a good place created by good Gods, and hatred of it does not bring ascension but only more ignominious rebirths. Such hatred is an understandable but improper reaction to the fact that in large part this plane is good *because* it is a place for souls to be cleansed and shepherded away from the nothingness they lust after, and such cleansing is sensationally painful like alcohol on a wound. As foolish as gnostic neurosis is, it is equally vital not to be lustfully attached to the material, and to remember that its goodness is rooted in what is above it.

The route to purification is to live virtuously and contemplatively. Our ancestors would contend that it is not possible to live virtuously without piety towards the Gods; who are we to question them? We see in the modern world that despite the mockery and the accusations of "slippery slope fallacy," and as stilted and inadequate as the religion of the last few centuries has been, people have in fact proven themselves even less virtuous without it.

To live with piety towards the gods in the modern age means to seek out and absorb as much information as you can about them in order to gain the knowledge necessary to act, and then to include the Gods in your daily life via prayers, offerings, and contemplation. In order to do this you may pick a couple gods, maybe one at a time, that you feel drawn to, focus on learning about them specifically, and then pray to them and give offerings if your circumstances allow. Finally, it must be said that this is a path much more easily walked with friends, and seeking out receptive people to share and develop your spiritual life with will prove highly rewarding and very helpful in your own pursuit of virtue.

What is a God?

This question is a tall order for the few pages available here. Nonetheless it is one that is very important for western polytheists to address in order to avoid chasing our tails trying to set up clean, clear divisions and equivalences between different gods both within single cultures and in the wider world, because these discussions often create more confusion than they clear up and can even introduce pointless animosities.

Let's begin defining gods first by what they are not. A god is not an egregore who is somehow "powered" by peoples' belief in them, though it may be the case that the strength of an individual's or community's faith can at times affect good luck, synchronicities, or even miracles. A god is not a mortal hero who has had stories about him embellished to the point that later generations believe him to be a god. Although divine heroes do abound and are an important part of the hellenic system of theology, what is divine in them is always *prior* to what is mortal in them. A god is not a personification or symbol of natural forces and processes, even though the gods undoubtedly make themselves known to us through nature. It is not right to say that Poseidon is a personified symbol of the sea. Instead we must consider the ocean as a living symbol, an icon, of the God whose activities on a higher plane are made apparent to us when our souls' memory is stirred by the witnessing of the rolling waves.

Now as for what a god *is*, there are many answers. The simplest answers, though, will be the most opaque to the novice: A god is a Oneness, a Goodness, a "Henad", and a god is a Cause, an unmoved mover. A God is a soul who exists beyond matter yet whose activities shape matter, a God is a nous who exists beyond soul and whose activities shape soul, and a God is a Oneness who exists beyond nous and who is beheld by the nous in worship, the activity through which the nous causes its descendents in soul and body to unfold.

While it is logically sound that the supreme principle of all reality and un-reality, The Good, Brahman, is One, it does not follow that there is only a singular God, a criticism levied against the Platonic and Vedic systems by both lazy monotheists and by certain polytheists who like wounded dogs are reflexively wary of the very concept of oneness. The possibility, and even necessity, of many Gods can be explained as such -

The supreme principle is that which individuates all things. Among these things are the very concepts of number and individuation, which the supreme principle must precede because it precedes all things which it individuates, which is everything. The supreme principle is therefore not *without* number, but it is *beyond* and unbound by number just like soul is beyond and unbound by matter. In fact the supreme principle must be unbound by anything which it contains, unbound by any category, and even unbound by the very concept of categories, including the category of "Gods." It is such an ineffable principle that the sages hesitate to try to speak of it, merely uttering the syllable "Om."

Nonetheless this principle is divine - or at least the category of "divinity" is the one which is nearest to encompassing it - and its light illumines the Gods and provides for them the "substance" out of which they unfold the rest of the cosmos like a telescoping pillar. Each God therefore is the demiurge of its own reality, even those like Dionysus or Herakles who exist already as members of a prior God's series. In fact all Gods exist in each others' series in some form, mutually reflecting each other like the dewdrops on Indra's net, though that comparison should not be taken too far. It is as members of these series which are suspended in the Gods that we as human souls have our existence and our subsistence, which we share with the rest of the cosmos from planets to algae. It is our privilege as noetic beings to be able to look upon and love the series in which we participate and all of those in which we are reflected, which is another form of participation.

The nature of the cosmos is as a sort of many-planed multiverse which is progressively unfolded from its most united state to its most divided. A god, in a sense, is what is left behind when the kaleidoscoping dance of forms collapses into a single united color. From their throne, where all things occur and are comprehended instantly and simultaneously, a god suffuses the things that we experience sequentially, divisibly, and limitedly by virtue of their unity.

The many levels of reality - the noetic, the psychic, and the physical being the primary ones that we know of - each receive divine light differently by virtue of the increasing granularity of the Forms. The result is that, within any single God's series, an abundance of gods stand at each level participating in what is above them and being participated in by what is below them. For example, Zeus exists celestially as Zeus, "aquatically" as Poseidon, "terrestrially" as Plouton, in the "sub-lunar" world as Dionysus, and in mankind himself as Herakles. Aphrodite exists transcendently as Ourania and imminently as Pandemos. Odin is Vili, Ve, and Oðr. Njorð suffuses his children Frey and Freya, so on and so forth.

Combined with the mutual participation of the Henads mentioned earlier, this is the reason that the devotee should not be overeager either to catalogue and divide the gods or to collapse them all into each other. An instance of Aphrodite exists in Ares and one of Ares exists in Aphrodite, yet both maintain their total self-oneness; i.e. Ares would still be Ares if, somehow, there were no Aphrodite for him to instantiate within, and vice-versa.

A God is in some ways like a prism which receives white light and sends forth a rainbow. It is common for worshippers to find a single god whom they most understand or are most connected to and then, when they draw closer to them, find that they see all possible divinity residing within their chosen (or fated) patron. Often they will conclude, because of this experience, that the God to which they are devoted represents the avatar of the highest principle itself. This is fine and normal; it is indubitable that if any god is a god at all, it must be fully god and fully divine, and one of the prime attributes of divinity is unity, unity which is shared by all divinity. So overwhelming and magnificent is the power of divinity that any contact at all can render mortals eager to admit the supremacy of whoever has afforded them such a privilege. Almost certainly this exact process occurred for the ancients as well and was responsible for things like the ascendancy of worship of Krishna, the Roman cult of Isis, the Orphic identification of Dionysus as supreme, and also - though political or perhaps demonic factors confound here - the emergence of Abrahamic monotheism out of the original semitic polytheist practices of the levant.

You may have noted the lack of language like "god of grain" or "god of wind" so far in this section. This might seem odd, because that's how we're used to hearing about pagan gods. The reason I am refraining from such language is that I want to make it clear that every god is first and foremost divine and conscious and the roles or attributes we use to describe them are not sufficient on their own to bring us towards them. It would be like trying to befriend a person by just reading their social media profile over and over without ever speaking to them. There will be valuable information that could increase your understanding or connection when the next step is taken, but the catalogues of epithets and duties are not the gods themselves, and it's important to be comfortable with mystery and with surface-level contradictions so that our gaze remains skyward instead of mired in details.

To be overzealous in categorizing and compartmentalizing the Gods risks flattening the mystical experience that their myths and symbols are meant to inspire. It's a very natural and normal impulse for newcomers and should be appreciated as a sign that the soul has recognized the direction in which it wants to move, but it's also a symptom of the attempt to grasp the divine with the discursive "bodily mind" which understands things by sorting, dismantling, and reconstructing them. The Gods will never yield to this mind, though, because they are beyond the purview of the things this mind is meant to do. The Gods are not a faucet to be fixed or a pulley to be constructed. Instead they must be witnessed with the eyes of the heart, eyes which have grown atrophied in many of us and which are even subtly mocked by the prevailing organizing principles of modern society, principles which are economic and inhuman.

The practice of religion is the practice of recovering that eyesight. I will attest with absolute certainty and from my own experience that the opening of the heart to these Gods is the opening of your deepest being to the entirety of life and the rousing of the self to become an active, subjective agent in its own activities and relationships instead of a sleepy stimulus-response machine. To trust the Gods is to walk with your guts hanging out and tasting the breeze. To relinquish unrighteous attachments, to relinquish them into the flames of sacrifice, is to make room for what is truly rewarding and nourishing.

In the end, the easiest and most relevant definition of a God that I can give you is this: A God is that which arrives when you call their name. The God is the reality which you enter when you are centered not in the chatter of the body but in the slow whalesong of worship, the clean silence of the purified altar and the gentle heat that is the gift of Vesta. A God will need no etymology, no venn diagrams, no history lesson, when they make themselves known. You will know who has come by the taste of their breath, and the proper name will spring to your mind like a childhood memory - because that is what it is.

Practicing Polytheism

There are many people who have an interest in the gods but feel that they have no clear entry point, no clear instructions on what to do or where to start. This is inevitable due to the current state of polytheism as a diverse set of different pantheons and traditions practiced by a very scattered selection of people with very little organization who communicate largely through the internet. Because of this diversity it can be difficult for a newcomer to find definitive information, and there even tends to be a sort of bias against "definitive-ness" among the often very open and non-conformist sorts of people that comprise modern polytheism. With all of that in mind, I'm going to quickly run through what I consider to be the very basic fundamental views and practices.

Western Polytheism, as a broad group of traditions, can be said to have three fundamental beliefs:

- Multiple Gods exist.

- These Gods have intellects and "persons" and engage in relationships with each other, humans, and the world.

- Religious practice exists as a symbol-complex reflecting truth like a mirror or lens which allows the embodied soul to approach it.

Likewise there are three pillars of practice:

- Always be learning and willing to engage with knowledge. Develop a desire for knowledge and for the knowledge of virtue.

- Empowered by such knowledge, participate in your relationships with the world, the gods, and other people virtuously.

- The practice of virtue in the self and its relationships then creates the proper environment for the fulfillment of the human telos as a social and divine creature.

The first belief is fairly simple: Multiple gods exist who are perfect, immortal, beyond material, and influence the universe in many different ways. Who these gods are, what they're like, and how they work are all very broad and complicated topics which will take a lifetime of work to unfold.

The second belief, naturally, relies on the first: These gods have intellects and "persons" and therefore participate in mutual relationships with each other and with all levels of reality, which includes human souls. Because humans have souls and intellects, we are able to discover the mutual bond of our soul with the gods and eventually participate in that bond intellectually and consciously.

The third belief is that religion, mythology, and symbology exists in order to aid us in that process of discovery. It is a symbol complex which reflects truth as a mirror reflects light. Almost all genuine religions reflect truth in some ways, but mirrors can be dirty. For us as westerners, the particular mirrors which we contend with are the Abrahamic traditions. It is clear that there is some truth present in them and that they are capable of producing virtuous people, but upon examination of their origins and histories it becomes evident that the social constructs built around their teachings must be categorically rejected as being dangerous political tools responsible for attacks on centuries of beauty and order in multiple civilizations. There is much more to say on this, but it must not sully the pages of a hymnal.

Although the Gods as beings are perfect and immortal, their religion on earth is constituted of symbology, imagery, rituality, and language. All of these things, even the names which we use to describe the Gods, are subject to mutation, decay, and generation. They are tools which our bodies and "bodily minds" use in order to construct an understandable reflection of the ineffable truth. Perhaps an apt but flawed metaphor would be to say that religion, mythology, and imagery act like very powerful sunglasses: Although the light of the sun is dimmed by them, without them you would not be able to look at the sun at all. You may be stuck squinting and staring at the ground forever.

This is an appropriate time to address the often raunchy or brutal nature of many of the myths that have survived to the present day. Such myths have resulted in many people coming to conceive of ancient religions as being morally licentious or inhumane, positions oddly maintained both by critics and by eager but immature proponents. While it is true that in some ways our conception of morality differs from that of the ancients, it's rarely a super severe discontinuity, and the apparent immoralities on display in the myths are usually acts of poetic license meant to communicate secret wisdom (though in the case of the received Norse mythology they are sometimes results of later christian tampering).

The Platonist Sallust says of myths:

> "Now the myths represent the Gods themselves and the goodness of the Gods - subject always to the distinction of the speakable and the unspeakable, the revealed and the unrevealed, that which is clear and that which is hidden: since, just as the Gods have made the goods of sense common to all, but those of intellect only to the wise, so the myths state the existence of Gods to all, but who and what they are only

to those who can understand. They also represent the activities of the Gods. For one may call the world a myth, in which bodies and things are visible, but souls and minds hidden. Besides, to wish to teach the whole truth about the Gods to all produces contempt in the foolish, because they cannot understand, and lack of zeal in the good, whereas to conceal the truth by myths prevents the contempt of the foolish, and compels the good to practice philosophy. But why have they put in the myths stories of adultery, robbery, father-binding, and all the other absurdity? Is not that perhaps a thing worthy of admiration, done so that by means of the visible absurdity the soul may immediately feel that the words are veils and believe the truth to be a mystery?

Of myths some are theological, some psychic, and some material, and some mixed from these last two. The theological are those myths which use no bodily form but contemplate the very essence of the Gods: e.g., Kronos swallowing his children. Since a god is intellectual, and all intellect returns into itself, this myth expresses in allegory the essence of a god. Myths may be regarded physically when they express the activities of the Gods in the world: e.g., people before now have regarded Kronos as time, and calling the divisions of time his sons say that the sons are swallowed by the father. The psychic way is to regard the activities of the soul itself; the soul's acts of thought, though they pass on to other objects, nevertheless remain inside their begetters. The mixed kind of myth may be seen in many instances: for example they say that in a banquet of the Gods Discord threw down a golden apple; the Goddesses contended for it, and were sent by Zeus to Paris to be judged. Paris saw Aphrodite to be beautiful and gave her the apple. Here the banquet signifies

21

the hypercosmic powers of the Gods; that is why they are all together. The golden apple is the world, which being formed out of opposites, is naturally said to be 'thrown by Discord'. The different Gods bestow different gifts upon the world, and are thus said to 'contend for the apple'. And the soul which lives according to sense - for that is what Paris is - not seeing the other powers in the world but only beauty, declares that the apple belongs to Aphrodite. Theological myths suit philosophers, physical and psychic suit poets, and mixed suit religious initiations, since every initiation aims at uniting us with the world and the Gods."

Now the discussion of belief is through and we may proceed to the practices. The first practice, like the first belief, is broad but still essential: You must always be learning, engaging with knowledge, and desiring to understand the world and its sustainers. It is a journey which may quite likely never end, but in its course you will encounter so many branching paths and revelations that it will be worth the effort anyway. This first practice is especially important in our position in the modern day because we find ourselves in a world that lacks widespread access to the most religiously relevant streams of godly knowledge that our ancestors would have had. At the same time we are uniquely privileged in that access to all that knowledge is still possible, it just takes digging and training and dedication.

Those requirements have so far meant that only particular sorts of people arrive at polytheism in the first place, and those who do arrive on occasion end up stagnating. Sometimes this is due to a lack of communal cohesion and direction, and other times the result of a failure to escape the moral presuppositions of secular materialism in order to embrace any sort of authentic traditional worldview that the men and women who once lived and breathed these practices would recognize. I will have more to say on that matter at another time, because solving it will be necessary if polytheism is going to outlive the anti-human secular regimes whose destruction of christianity have ironically allowed western dharmic traditions to reemerge in the first place.

Through the first of our practices, learning, we attain the knowledge of how to carry out the second practice, which relates to something known as the gifting cycle: You must participate in your bonds and relationships honorably, both with humans and with Gods. Again, this is a broad and diverse topic, but very basic and foundational rules often must be. The broadness of this rule derives from the fact that different sorts of relationships require different approaches; even though we wish to cultivate *eros,* "compulsion towards beauty," both with our human community and with the Gods, the correct ways of doing so are different. Likewise, we treat with "Ouranic" (Olympian, or "heaven-dwelling") Gods in a different manner than we do with "Chthonic" (Earthly or subterranean) Gods such as Pluto, and there are still other practices for treating with local spirits/genii, lares, deceased ancestors, or ascended Heroes such as Achilles, Alexander, or Julian. This second practice is the one which encompasses the majority of ritual, ethical, and communal protocol.

The third practice is to always be seeking after virtue and self-perfection in your words, deeds, thoughts, and actions. It sounds like a high bar, but it's really not: Here, as with the first practice, the point is to try more so than to succeed. Many small successes await you on the path towards this lofty aim, and you will never regret trying unless you set unreasonable expectations, which the god Krishna warns us against in the *Bhagavad Gita:*

"You have the right to work, but for the work's sake only. You have no right to the fruits of work. Desire for the fruits of work must never be your motive in working. Never give way to laziness, either. Perform every action with your heart fixed on the Supreme Lord (Krishna). Renounce attachment to the fruits. Be even-tempered in success and failure: for it is this evenness of temper which is meant by yoga. Work done with anxiety about results is far inferior to work done without such anxiety, in the calm of self-surrender. Seek refuge in the knowledge of Brahma. They who work selfishly for results are miserable."

In the pursuit of this aim, that first practice of seeking after knowledge is again supremely important. That may be obvious. What may be less obvious, though, is that the second practice of carrying out our relationships properly is also vital here. So vital, in fact, that I could have chosen to subsume this practice under that one if I did not believe that it warranted its own detailed treatment and emphasis. The reason I say that is because the pursuit of personal perfection and improvement can only be carried out once an individual learns to *cultivate and practice a good relationship with his or her self.*

The object of the witnessed "self," after all, is a dynamic structure which emerges out of the interaction of many forces just like a community does - or the cosmos, for that matter. Let us briefly examine Plato's theory of soul. Plato teaches that the soul, the "psyche" (ψυχή), is divided into three portions:

- Logos - The head, the faculty of reason and thought, and the charioteer in his allegory of the soul.

24

- Thumos - The heart and solar plexus, the Will, the spirit, and the white horse of his allegory.

- Epithymetikon - "Appetite," desire and aversion, the belly and genitalia, and the black horse of his allegory.

When these three portions are balanced with each other, the result is a life which is harmonious no matter what outside events occur. Sickness and distress often come from imbalance or disharmony between these parts of the self, but remedying such imbalance can be very difficult because when we press against any one part in order to reshape it and bring it into harmony with the other parts, we experience pain thanks to identifying with the part we are pressing against just as much as we identify with the other parts of our self which that part is harming. A simple example: It's very easy to become slothful, which happens when our appetite loves ease and comfort and gains too much power. This imbalance tyrannizes over the parts of ourselves which love action, advancement, order, and triumph.

In the course of trying to overcome sloth, a person will frequently want to give up, saying "*I* don't care, *I* don't want to do this, this is too difficult for *me*." The "I" which is speaking in those moments is the unharmonious self, the sloth-tyrannized self, and if that person gives in to that self then discontent will only grow. The appetite cannot satisfy itself because it is incomplete without Thumos and Logos, and so when it becomes unbalanced it harms *itself* as well.

I use this tyranny of the appetite as an example because it is one of the most common imbalances among humans, both in our day and in Plato's. In our philosophical canon there is a lot of negative discussion of the Appetite, but that is merely due to the tendency of that part of the soul to be the most common "problem area" for humans. That makes sense, as it is the most basal of the three parts and the nearest to the material world. It is a necessary and good part of us, though; the proper attitude towards the appetite is gentle guidance, to listen to it but not to give it final say.

There are many similar three-part splits in traditions all across the world, often sharing an Indo-European origin. The significance and usefulness of the Platonic model of the soul is that it gives us a good basic map of what the self is and how it interacts with its own parts. Having such a map is the first step in gaining that mastery over the self which enables us to pursue the third practice. If we are not allowing our higher selves to guide our actions, we will not increase in the virtues which allow us to learn and grow and to fulfill our relationships rightly. Each of the three practices rely on each other for their own fulfillment, just as the three parts of the soul do.

When we identify with and empower our logos and our better judgement, we are drawn "upwards," into further likeness with the Gods, as like attracts like. When we fail to do this, we do not have to say we are drawn towards "evil" or that we are punished or condemned, but our true selves do become "diluted" by our own actions, and our higher self experiences that state of fogginess, powerlessness, and distance from the Gods as suffering.

The three beliefs exist in order to provide your mind with a space, a horizon, a toolkit, in which you can exercise the three practices. The stories, images, and philosophical understandings of the Gods which we have inherited are things of immense beauty. When it is understood that such things are rooted in a fundamental reality which is greater than (but still subsumes and interacts with) matter, and when self-mastery towards the goal of virtue is practiced, we attain the frame of mind that allowed our forebears to create civilizations that still shape who we are today. More importantly, we attain the frame of mind which allowed them to live lives so overflowing with power and sincerity that it would seem absurd to the malnourished and deprived people that today find themselves trapped in a world of anxiety, overstimulation, and helplessness.

The aspect of practice which is most relevant to us right now for this project is that of prayer and sacrifice, which can be taught with the terms of the "gifting cycle." This is a phrase I've borrowed from heathenry, whose tendency to place a strong emphasis on morality and community I admire. The "gifting cycle" refers to exchange between man and the gods, but also between humans themselves. The exchange of both physical and intangible gifts such as food, affection, support, wealth, and aid is the process which is responsible for creating the bonds between people that make community and communal life possible. This practice has equivalents in nearly every Indo-European tradition we know of, as well as most other culture groups' indigenous polytheisms.

In the same way that bonds between people create a human community, bonds between the Gods and the primordial substances of being create the cosmos. That might not be an adequately precise way to word it, as "substance" and "being" are pretty loaded terms philosophically and endless arguments can be had over this sort of thing, but we're going to learn to crawl before we can run. If we're successful, then someday more virtuous people than us can argue about it while reclining next to a vestal hearth. The important thing, at any rate, is that the Gods are engaged in a process of offering their own affection, talents, and substance to the world, to each other, and to us. Emulating that process with ourselves, our community, and our environment is therefore

27

an important part of becoming like the gods and living rightly.

Just as we form bonds with humans by investing time, effort, and material, when we invest time, effort, or material into learning about the Gods and acting righteously we transform our relationship to them. They give many gifts to us constantly and thanklessly; life, happiness, and love are all given even to people with no consciously cultivated relationships to any gods (though it could be argued that these gifts, or at least the gracious conscious reception of them, are all diminished when atheism occurs both at the societal and individual scales). When we dedicate our own substance to the Gods by learning, acting, and offering worship, we change from being passive recipients of gifts we don't understand or appreciate into being affirmative and willing participants in a cycle of exchange which improves our lives and our selves. This is not a matter of "enslaving" ourselves to the Gods as some neopagans might complain; to suggest our subordination to the Gods is unjust or optional is akin to saying that a person "enslaves" their fingers and toes when he moves them. Participating willingly in the gifting process is a step away from slavery, not towards it, because through it we begin to share the sovereignty of the Gods rather than letting it exert itself over our lives without us ever knowing.

When polytheists use images and statues in worship, it is understood that these icons serve as symbolic objects that help to anchor our physical, animal selves to our worship by granting our eyes an image to associate with the incorporeal forces that are being engaged. Similarly, when we offer food, drink, or votive objects like weapons or jewelry, what is being exchanged is not the physical matter of those items but rather the powers that are symbolically vested in them; food is strength and sustenance, drink can be purity, merriment, or revelation, and various other objects carry different meanings.

The use of those items serves a similar purpose to the use of an icon: It forms mental connections between the motions of the physical body and spiritual phenomena. Our stomachs already know firsthand of the nourishing power of food, and so when we symbolically return that nourishing force to the Gods through offerings the action is understood in a more physically holistic way. In a sense, we are sublimating our bonds with the experiences of hunger, fulfillment, purification, strength, or whatever else is vested in the offered items, into a bond with the worshipped God. That bond already existed and would exist regardless of practice simply because of the nature of the Gods and our position relative to them, but the ritual process of creating a way for our minds and bodies to perceive and contribute to that bond is perhaps the first and most vital step in establishing religious practice. All subsequent religious engagement happens as a part of the gifting cycle. The process can wax and wane as life goes on, but it is always the basis of our relationships, and relationships are the basis of existence both for man as a social animal and for the cosmos as a series of bonds between different forces and Gods.

Turning this concept into practice in worship is pretty easy. It is simply done through prayer and offering. Prayer can run the gamut of complexity from a single sentence to a long "conversation" and can be spoken alone or as part of other practices like meditation and the offering-rite itself. A prayer is composed of at least two elements, the invocation and the petition, though they can be as elaborate as necessary. A proper posture is not strictly necessary, but you will find it helpful to pray with your palms facing upwards and your eyes fixed either towards the sky if outdoors or on the flame if indoors. If addressing "chthonic" deities or aspects, i.e. gods whose roles revolve around death or the underworld such as Plouton and Persephone, your palms should face towards the ground and your eyes be straight and level.

The invocation is the recital of the names, titles, roles, attributes, or feats of the addressed God. It can be as short as "Lady Athena" or as elaborate as "Lady Athena, Euboulaia, warden of cities, you who guided the hand of Odysseus." Its purpose is ostensibly to call the attention of the deity, though it also gathers the mind to focus itself on the god. While it is true that where the mind goes the tongue will follow, it is also true that when the tongue speaks the mind will take up its words.

The petition which follows is the meat of the prayer and where the actual intention is declared. "Petition" is an imperfect term for it, because it's not just about requests. The petition can be asking for something, yes, but when things like money or particular events are requested then results should not be expected or relied upon due to the nature of fate and the mortal potential for misalignment of priorities between the layers of the self. The best requests to make to the gods are for spiritual or intangible things; to help one become more patient, persistent, kind, satisfied, at peace, etc. Often those are the things which our deepest selves really *mean* to ask for when we think we desire things like money, because physical things operate as symbolic stand-ins for the states of being they induce, states like calmness and independence. Part of the point of developing selfhood and subsistence in the Gods, though, is becoming able to induce states like bliss, openness, and oneness without an external or physical stimulus. Nonetheless it would be hard to craft a "bad" prayer, and you should feel free to speak to the divine often, about anything, and without fear or reservation.

To give examples of the different request petitions, we will continue the prayer begun above. The first and most basic sort might read thus:

"Lady Athena, may you grant me victory."

The latter and more refined sort, meanwhile, might read like this:

"Lady Athena, may you help me to act bravely, wisely, with my mind fixed upon you, and in this way attain victory."

Both are fine prayers, both are good. Both will be heard and, in one way or another, answered. The primary difference lies in the fact that the second prayer better clarifies for our own mind what we should expect from the Goddess according to the laws of this world and of virtue and precludes us from whatever unrighteous disillusionment we might inflict on ourselves if the immediate, tangible victory requested in the first prayer was not fated.

The petition is also often simply a declaration of adoration or, the best prayer of all, gratitude. For example, "Lord Thor, I thank you for your protection", or "Lady Freya, most beautiful goddess, may you accept my praise." Such prayers are excellent because they point directly to the prime objective of worship, which is not to enact worldly change (though that also happens and is good) but to bring the soul into line with its divine origin through devotion and the opening of pathways of love and mutual recognition. If a prayer request is fulfilled, then it is paramount to offer thanks. Often requests will be fulfilled for the express purpose of providing you with a reminder, an occasion, an "excuse" to practice gratitude and adoration. Like begets like, and so the mind which is immersed in gratitude and adoration, training itself in the witnessing of the good, brings more good to itself, as is the will of the gods.

Without gratitude, adoration, and the unity they beget, the mind is prone to lose itself in the nihilism of fear and lust which are always as a rule anchored in what one does not possess or what is not real. Even so, these compulsions are still rooted in the mind's desire for goodness. The heart wills to lack bad things and to possess good things, but without knowledge of the gods and of virtue it is deceived by the senses as to what is truly good for it in the long term (eternity being a very long term indeed). The attachment of the bodily mind to worldly things is why worldly prayer-requests have efficacy, because providence extends through all things, even down into matter, regardless of how diluted it may become. That is also the mechanism by which religious language and imagery holds power.

Prayer is as much for us as for the gods. It is a human activity, but it is pleasing to them. This is not because they require attention or because it somehow fuels their ego. It is simply because prayer is good for us, helping us to perfect ourselves, and this is pleasing to the gods because we reside in them and their love for us and for the world is a self-love. We may even consider the Gods themselves to live in a constant state of prayer, fixing their manifold eyes upon all things and upon all their fellows and extolling their goodness and the oneness which they share with the supreme principle.

Now that prayer has been discussed, we must briefly touch on ritual and offerings. This will be simpler than prayer but not necessarily easier. Experienced polytheists, feel free to skip ahead.

Traditionally an offering rite requires only a few things: A clean (and purified) space, a flame or light, and an offering. Many people take great pride and pleasure in creating and beautifying a dedicated altar, and I encourage this, but strictly speaking it is only necessary to set out a flat space and to cleanse the surrounding area as well as one's hands and face. This can be done with a simple washing or with holy water, which is created by combining water, salt, and burnt plant matter like an herb, leaf, or twig. Once this is done and the flame is lit, the devotee invokes and offers to a gateway god such as Hestia, Janus, Hermes, Odin, Heimdall, or Agni in order to begin the offering in earnest. After this you may address with prayer and offer to whichever gods you wish or whoever is most appropriate to the current situation, and then finish the ritual by again offering to the gateway god.

For a drink offering or poured libation, simply pour the liquid into a receptacle and declare the intention that it is an offering, for example by stating "Hestia, may you accept this offering." The liquid can be anything really, with water, milk, and alcohol being the most traditional offerings. If it is a solid offering, such as food, jewelry, etc, simply place it on the altar with the same declaration. For "skyward" or Ouranic deities, which are most deities, you may consume the offering after concluding the ritual, though it is not necessary. For chthonic deities the offering should not be consumed, and generally drink offerings to them should also be poured out onto the ground and solid offerings buried.

An offering can take any form, such as an icon or idol or just a nice mug, really anything that you attach importance or enjoyment to, because that attachment is the source of its efficacy in directing our mortal attention and intentions. Think of it in terms of hospitality: Through prayer and ritual we "invite the gods into our lives" by establishing conscious acknowledgment of their works, and so it is customary to welcome them with gifts. In return, they invite us into their own abode with unity and with momentary respite from the onslaught of time and change. Thus the gifting cycle is fulfilled and the fickle wheel of fortune stilled through the experience of non-duality that is birthed in the act of giving, a generosity that is an imitation of the very generosity and superabundance that causes the Good and the Gods to unfold into the rest of the world.

With all of this in mind, it is nearly time for the actual hymns and prayers of this book. My hope is that they will be enjoyable to you and help you to approach and understand these gods, but I also hope that you will come into this book as a participant rather than just a reader. My intention is that this book will be able to help transform the Gods from things that are studied into realities that are experienced. Towards this end, in the print version, I've included a lined journal page in each god's section that I hope you will take advantage of to write down your thoughts on each god, what in your life you are thankful to them for, and prayers of your own composition for ritual use.

Unfortunately there are many gods who have not been included in this book, and though I fully intend to address them in future editions as well as expanding the scope of future works to include the Celtic, Egyptian, Persian, and Babylonian names and ways of approaching the Gods, I hope that those of you whose favored gods are absent will still be able to gain good insight and deepen your practice with the help of these hymns. As a final disclaimer I will note that this work is heavily informed by a personal practice which is strongly colored by Orphic Platonism and by Vedanta. I am convinced there is adequate truth to it - I wouldn't publish this if I wasn't - but I do anticipate and welcome disagreement and don't wish to cast this work as infallibly authoritative. My concern is not historical or academic but religious, and adequately communicating such things is always fraught with the risk of misunderstanding or mistranslation.

Now, to conclude: The sensation of worship, when it finally clicks, can be like sliding into a hot bath or like stepping through the door on a windy day. For many of us, as inundated in technology and notifications and distractions as we are, to finally have our attention commanded so forcefully by something that does not flash or beep or jiggle can be just as alien as it is deeply transformative. And yet this is when we are most fully ourselves, because our selfhood exists *in* and *through* and *from* the Gods.

Whether you are arriving here as a history enthusiast, a spiritual seeker, a student of magic, a curious infidel, or a fellow devoted pagan, I am sure that the paths which have led you here are strange and entertaining. May we raise the mixing-bowl to them, may we share these prayers, and may Artemis light your steps by night as surely as Apollo does by day.

Zeus

Jupiter, Jove, Dias

Zeus is many things. Zeus is even many Gods. Zeus, due to his position as king of the gods, is in a way the "God of Gods" or the "God of God-ness," being the reality whose mutual participation ensures the divinity of all gods. This may be partly a matter of perspective that lingers in the tradition from its early developmental stages when, drawing near to the Sky Father and Striker due to his relevance to their pastoral lives, the ancients adopted him as chief deity.

As discussed in the introduction, ancient peoples were so diverse in space and time that the perspective of which God was primary could fluctuate. Perspectives could even cohabitate with others when individual cults, which sometimes approached monolatry, are taken into account.

Generally, though, whichever god is considered chief would be assigned some similar attributes, and for the purpose of concision I will discuss them here as attributes of Zeus (most of which also extend to his northern theophany, Odin).

The King of the Gods is the one in whom the ineffable supreme principle makes itself most symbolically legible and unimpeded. With Zeus, this is seen in his fondness for vastness and openness and for prolific generation and attraction. He is mythologically portrayed as having great care and empathy for his progeny, but also as frequently being bound by oath or natural order (things that are also his descendants) to withhold his aid and allow the tutelary drama to unfold.

It is because of that generosity that Zeus is connected astrologically to the planet Jupiter, though he is also very solar, specifically in his role as the first of several gods who serve to create and bridge different levels of reality by projecting the higher into the lower. Zeus serves as the foundation of all things by projecting the ineffable supreme principle of the One as accurately as structurally possible into the space that arises from the interaction of the Forms of "Infinity" and "Boundary," thus giving rise to Being in the positive, affirmative sense.

As concerns the more immediate needs of the lay devotee, there is really very little in life that Zeus isn't relevant to, and calling to him is never going to be unjustified. The things with which he is especially concerned, though, are as such:

Firstly, he is concerned with all things familial, fatherhood and marriage especially. This is because, in the pagan ethos, all the world is viewed as participating in the familial clan dynamic of the Gods. This will be treated on more extensively with Hera.

Secondly, Zeus presides over our reconciliation with fate and with that which is outside of or opposed to ourselves. As we will see with Dionysus and Herakles, ultimately he aims to do this by dissolving our illusion of separation from these things and from himself, but until that realization occurs he is content to mediate through Law and through encouraging the cultivation of virtue, Arete. Honor him by seeking to be virtuous and even-handed in your dealings with other people and with the world in general.

Thirdly, Zeus is a protector and purifier. The rain washes as much as it nourishes, and the thunder strikes down what is unclean - a function strongly emphasized in worship of Thor. Sometimes, though, because of Zeus' responsibility to the whole world and to its ordering, which often requires compromise, the devotee may choose "closer" Gods like Herakles or Athena for protective purposes.

The Orphic hymns which you are about to read and which feature prominently in this book emphasize Zeus' inescapable all-pervasiveness, to the point that hymns to many other gods will directly call that god "a Zeus" or "the Zeus." As touched on in the introduction, that should not be taken as diminishing those gods nor as de-individualizing Zeus but rather as aggrandizing them and super-individuating Zeus as one who is simultaneously One and Many because he is rooted beyond the point at which those labels acquire any meaning or opposition to each other.

And now, Father Zeus, may you come to hear our prayers and be pleased by them.

Orphic Rhapsodic Hymn to Zeus

Zeus! The first and last and Lord
Of bright-tipped lightning,
Zeus the Head and Center, all things
Come to be from Zeus' mind

Zeus comes forth as male,
Deathless Zeus comes as a nymph,
And Zeus is the foundation
Of the broad green earth and starry sky

Zeus is sovereign over all, Zeus is all things' cause,
Highest godhood, Emperor, one power and one mind,
And one royal body containing the course
Of all the spinning heavens

Fire, Water, Earth, and Aither, Nyx, Eos, and Day,
With first-begotten Metis and with Eros' gentle ways
Are all within Olympian Zeus
As Sun contains his rays

Behold His head with handsome face, effulgent daylit Sky,
He crowns himself with stars by night
And wears those Taurine horns-
The rising and setting roads of the Sun,
The pathways walked by Gods

His eyes are blessed Helios and lovely bright Selene,
His mind is royal truth itself, bounding all the aither,
Hearing All and contemplating;
No word nor cry nor prayer nor even anything which Is
Escapes the ear of Kronos' son.

Immortal mind, immortal head,
And boundless shining body, unvexable
With broad and fearless arms, exceeding might
In the shoulders and chest and rippling back
Of the God whose form is swirling air

Winged god, flying here and there,
With the whole wide matronly Earth for His gut
With her hills and mountains,
And deep-roaring Ocean for His belt
With His feet, those stout foundations,
Planted deep in Tartarus

Hiding all things and bringing them forth,
Newly birthed in delightful vision,
Again and again from His own heart He brings them,
Acting with joy and in awe of Himself

Orphic Hymn 15 - Zeus

Zeus, Highly honored, invincible God,
We offer our prayers, redeemer and cleanser,
Basileios whose crown brings light
To all that is divine and clear

Mother Earth and towering mountains
And the sea and swirling stars
Array themselves in harmony
Beneath your thundering scepter

Saturnian Jove, come clothed in the lightning,
Strong-hearted God, come wielding Thunder,
Uniter, creator, beginning and end,
Pantokrator, Father, Increaser, World-Shaker,

Purifying, nourishing, hear us God,
Sustaining life with many forms,
May you grant us spotless health
And with Eirene on your arm
Send peace and wealth with cheerful honor

Orphic Hymn 19 - Thundering Zeus

Father Zeus, how sublime is the course which you drive
Through the fiery stars as they shrink from your might,
Lofty, aithereal, bottomless thundering
Shakes all the seats of the heavenly thrones

The blaze of your fulmen illumines the rainclouds,
You drive storms and tempests and tireless gales,
Hurling the torrent of shrieking bolts;
Might and horror, burning missiles,
Pounding hearts and raising hairs to bristle

Holy and invincible, Sudden crash and endless spiral,
Driving, unbreakable, booming, consuming,
Irresistibly sharp smoking shafts of the gale,
Swooping down with fearful flashes,
Your celestial thunder's rolling shine is mirrored
In the eyes of men and routing beasts

O blessed God who wields the thunder,
Shredding heaven's silken girdle,
The furious waves and the stout windy summits
Bear witness to you, acclaiming you Lord

So may you, O God, receive in your power
The prayers and gifts which we give in your honor,
May you nurture our youths and, from your own abundance,
Grant lives ever-blooming with health and with cheer,
Blooming with wealth and with thoughts free of fear

Orphic Hymn 20 - Zeus Astrapaios

I call upon you, great and pure,
Resounding and illustrious,
You whose blazing, rushing fire
Shines through the aither and flashes in clouds
With the ear-splitting crash of the striker and victor

Incomparable God, wrathful and pure,
I call upon you, lord of lightning,
All-father, ruler, Basileios, judge,
May you look upon me kindly,
And make my life's end proud and sweet

Hymn to Zeus of the Firmament

You are vaulted heaven, white horizon Your wide grin
And all the clouds Your teeth, stained with sorrow's marrow -
O God who tastes these best, do tell
Your sons how futile tears must be
When every breath is joy to You,
And sings Your highest praise
Both from the chests of lions
And the bubbling throats of prey

For You are all the rounded spheres and every firmament
Is circled in Your one wide gut,
Blue with thunder - rolling laughter!
Wide arms wring out Rhea's daughter.

Hymn to Sovereign Zeus

Mighty Zeus who wields the thunder,
Vaulted heaven's holy keeper,
Father God who holds the scepter,
Rightly-judging wide-armed ruler

All within the Olympian One
Are as daughters to you, and sons,
And Each within the Olympian All
Kneels to you and heeds your call;

Let us sing of the gifts which you graciously give,
The rain and the lighting, that sunlight which lives
In the centers of seeds and the organs of beasts
And the wine that we offer at all of your feasts

For you are the one who Is and who rules,
Protector of kings and of wandering fools,
So when we are lost, may you grant us safe travels
And when we are found, help us build up your temples

Zeus' Xenia Prayer

High Olympian Zeus, God and master over all,
Great divine upholder of the oaths of hospitality,
May you open up my heart and home
To any who would grace it,
Yet ward away and vanquish those
Who have no ruth or honor

Zeus' Inspiration Prayer

Father Zeus, source of All, Fountain, King, and shaper,
May you hear my faithful prayer
And drive me forth with inspiration,
Boundless will to do my duties,
And a fruitful mind which shares creation

Odin

Oðinn, Wotan, Woden

Odin is by far the most attested and treated-on god known from the remaining sources of ancient Germanic and Norse religion. Works of comparative religion addressing him seem to have more luck with measuring him against Hindu deifics than Hellenic ones, but it is nonetheless clear that he neatly fills the role of cosmic creator-god and, as succinctly put by his own cult, "Allfather."

What is perhaps most illuminating in his mythography is his co-creation of the world with his "brothers" Vili and Ve, his relationship with the world-tree Yggdrasil, and his self-sacrifice to gain the knowledge of the runes.

In the beginning, the primeval cow Audhumla licked the giant Buri out of a glacier. Buri, the first intellective being, then begat Bor who begat Odin, Vili, and Ve. The three brothers then slew the ice-giant Ymir and created the world from his body. Ymir is emblematic of unformed, "empty" matter, which the three gods possess the power to shape and overcome because of their noetic heritage.

We must remember here the concept of "mythic time": Ymir has not ceased to exist and been partitioned at a particular historic point, but he exists continually and the process of the Gods creating the world out of him is happening perpetually and omni-simultaneously.

The name "Odin" means "Inspiration," "Vili" means "Will," and "Ve" means "Holiness." It is clear that these are meant to be the three faculties of the creator-god that are primarily responsible for creation: Inspiration brings the higher into the lower, and Will compels the projected substance to be ordered. Finally, and most cryptically, Ve refers to holiness in the sense that a thing outside of the self is recognized as sacred and in turn compels the viewer to greater self-knowledge. The concept of darśana is relevent here.

In sum, the creation myth teaches us this: The supreme principle of being and non-being unfolds into positive being when the numinous power firstly beholds it, then attaches value and will to it, and then beholds himself in his new creation, the beholding of himself being a second and refracted beholding of the initial principle, which explains the fractal and trinitary nature of existence and of the gods.

Yggdrasil, the world tree, is actually Odin's eight-legged horse Sleipnir; "Ygg-drasil" translates to "The steed of Ygg," Ygg being an epithet of Odin. That Odin both lives within the world-tree and rides upon it is indicative of the simultaneous transcendance and immanence of godhead. Sleipnir seems to be the preferred method of traversal into and out of Helheim for the living. This is congruent with the general symbolic association of horses as being mighty beasts but quite intertwined with the world of generation and decay as is seen in Poseidon's patronage of them. Horses also indicate travel, which connects to the final myth we'll be treating on.

For nine days and nine nights, Odin hanged himself on the world-tree, a sacrifice in order to earn knowledge of the runes, the secrets of creation and perhaps analogous to the Platonic Forms. The Runes are the specific notes or vibrations that contribute to the song of creation as extracted from Ymir's corpse. On the world-axis, which is also his steed and even his spear Gungnir, Odin stretched himself from the highest to the lowest and, through self-contemplation, deduced the structural principles of the cosmos and the proper magical and linguistic method of representing them. Thus it is through union with him that poetry, philosophy, science, medicine, and theology are made possible to mankind.

Yet for all his luminosity and lofty consciousness, Odin can remain quite opaque to the devotee. Possibly, as with Hera and as described by Sallust's excerpt on mythology, this is intended to spur the student to action and contemplation, a trick of "reverse psychology." Certainly Odin encourages and rewards curiosity, cleverness, and bravery.

In practical, everyday worship, Odin rules the pursuit of knowledge, self-perfection (including health), and victory. Honor him by devoting yourself to these. This may at first seem a narrow domain for the king of creation, but contemplation will reveal that it is a never-ending quest which is always exerting its demands upon you.

May Father Odin now come to hear our prayers, and may he judge them rightly and kindly.

Hymn to Runeseeking Odin

Nine days rounding the circle,
Yourself to Yourself, blood exits
Where gungnir enters,
The serpent bites its tail.

Nine worlds rounding the circle,
You travel seeking
Wisdom in your own vast corners:

"I am frenzy
In love and war,
In song and dance and
In death and birth I am

The Will feeding itself
With rage and joy-
Swallow my eye!
One vision gathers the spheres"

Hymn to Father Wotan

You raise us up an altar
Out of every Ash and Oak
And etch your runesong in the roots
Which found and feed and clothe your folk

Kingdoms nine you rule and judge,
Rule you kingdoms nine,
Guiding each by numen-sight
Afforded to your single eye

Wotan, Vili, Ve, we call you
From your triple throne
To guide and teach your mortal sons
And sanctify our homes

Hymn to the Runatyr

Odin's frenzied zenith spins
With dizzy strength, effulgence leaks
Into the blood, the thick, bright blood

The blood of honeyed poetry
Pulsing thick in crashing waves,
Yggr-snake unfurls to taste the soma drink

Ghostly wisdom's subtle stream
In branches, breath, and sunny breeze
Spirals up to hail and join the all-begetting Runatyr

Woden's Prayer for Wisdom

Father Woden, World-Walker, All-Seer,
You have travelled seeking knowledge
And the ways of righteous living;
May you, great God, instruct me in these things,
And grant me waxing wisdom always.

Woden's Oðr Prayer

Raging, flying, far-surpassing,winner of the Runes,
Wandering father seeking truth, Zealous King and Priest,
May you ignite my thirst for wisdom and for rightful action
And make my travels overflow with godly inspiration,
As sweet and as abundant as your dripping horn of mead

Woden's Prayer for Healing

Bone to Bone and Flesh to Flesh
May you bind and prosper, God,
Father, Seeker, Teacher, Healer,
Blessed Woden, hear my prayer
And gently tend your child's wounds

Hera

Juno, Dione, Kronia

Hera is perhaps the most cultiurally underappreciated Olympian relative to her role. She is the queen of heaven, the Goddess of Goddesses just as Zeus is God of Gods. She is closely intertwined with her father Kronos, being a strongly intellective or noetic force. She, beholding the oneness of her husband Zeus and wishing to proliferate it, is the enactor of multiplicity, which is not an absence of oneness but an elaborating and complicating superabundance of it. She gives rise to the eminent force of femininity just as Zeus does masculinity, as femininity is traditionally associated with multiplication, elaboration, dis- and re-unification, and regulation.

Hera's involvement in that first process is symbolized by her patronage of childbirth. The second and third processes are seen in her interactions with Herakles, who she drives to accomplish great deeds and who is eventually reunited with his divine origin and reconciled to Hera herself by his marriage to Hebe, a youthful hypostasis of Hera. The fourth and final process, regulation, is seen in Hera's, and especially the Roman Juno's, involvement in the processes of law and sovereignty, which are extensions and extrapolations of the clan matriarch's duties onto the scale of a wider society, which is rightly viewed as a fractally extending family.

Hera is the first hypostasis of the Animating Triad, consisting of herself, Demeter, and Artemis. Where Demeter unfolds Life into separate lives and Artemis Intellect into seperate minds, Hera unfolds Being at its most fundamental, Jovian level into the plurality of beings. As the first unfolder she makes all "posterior" unfoldings possible and establishes the laws through which all plural things relate to each other, the laws of physics, of karma, and of the state being a few examples.

Because of this one of her primary symbols is the Peacock, whose tail wears the hundred eyes of Argus and is remniscent of the omni-mutual beholding and refracting of Indra's net. This is her fundamental and paradoxical mystery, the non-contradiction of oneness and many-ness that seems to set her in conflict with her husband but which is in fact a product of her unity with him.

Establishing plurality and boundary, Hera can seem challenging and unforgiving. That challenge, though, is her gift to us, and proper navigation of it leads to the highest rewards.

The Basileia's symbols include a golden throne, the pomegranate, the lotus, and the lion. The devotee should entreat her in matters of family or matters that require mediation, and should also take care to remember her when faced with challenges and to accept them as her gift. She draws things out into plurality and sets them in their rightful relationships, which sometimes appear antagonistic. This process, which is continued and perfected by Aphrodite and Ares, is meant to alchemically draw out the best from each-soul as it undertakes its journey. Again paradoxically, what appears messy or antagonistic becomes generative and puri-fying. More will be said about that when we entreat Herakles.

Astrologically, Hera is intertwined with Saturn and with the seemingly incongruous constellations of Cancer and Aquarius. Cancer, which begins in her month of June, con-cerns the household and its boundaries, while atmospheric and Saturnian Aquarius concerns the negotiation of thought and law amidst masses of people where abstraction and de-personalization are necessary.

To the devotee she may be aloof, but underpinning that is a sense of supreme peace and regality. One may also be concerned about her judgement, but you should rest assured that whatever is asked of you is asked for your own sake. Hera seeks your perfection and reunion as much as any god does, and she is willing to be insenstive about it. Honor her by cultivating justice, decisiveness, and clarity.

And now, Mother Hera, may you hear the prayers of your devotees and look mercifully on them.

Orphic Hymn 14 - Hera

Air-formed Hera, caerulean throned,
Empress of All, beloved of Zeus,
Essence itself your gentle breath,
A breeze blown into empty space

Mother of winds, mother of rains,
Attendant of the fruitful storm,
There is no life without you,
And nowhere are you absent;

Not in the skies and not on the earth,
Not amidst waves or the slow-moving mountains,
Not in the hearths of the clan or of spouses,
Never does anything lack you, Regina

Sovereign, Basileia, stately one,
May you, the course of swirling stars,
Come now with your thousand names to hear
Our thanks, and our praise, and our pleas.

Hymn to Kronian Hera

Teach us, Goddess, how the stars
Can all themselves be suns,
And teach us, Hera, how the world
Is many, yet is one

The peacock's dashing tail
Dressed in Argus' hundred eyes
Tells us of your power,
Of the Queen of Heaven's pride

For in your vast and snow-white arms
You wield multiplicity,
The power to draw out the many from one
And return them all to simplicity

As families are wives and husbands and youths,
The clan is a family of hearths,
And you are the power of union and oath
Who binds our childish hearts

You bind them to spouses and offspring,
You bind them to states and their laws,
But most of all you bind them
To the gifts and the works of the Gods

So come, Basileia, with cool windy breath
To take up our praises and prayers,
Come bearing a sovereign mind and pure heart
To bring strength, life, and law to our heirs

Zeus and Hera's Gamos Prayer

Peerless Zeus and Hera,
Joined in blessed theogamia,
With heaven as your marriage bed
You rule from vast Olympus.

All the cosmos is your clan,
And You our blessed elders;
May you make our family's bonds
As strong as golden chain

Hera's Concord Prayer

Mother Hera, Counselor,
With far-surpassing sovereign mind
As wide as your rushing, swirling sky,
May you preserve our understandings, aid us in diplomacy,
And uphold peace in all the bonds
That form the family, tribe, and state

Hebe's Prayer

Gentle Hebe, golden-throned, bearer of the nectar-cup,
Daughter of the Queen of Heaven, Daughter of the King,
And bride of thundering Herakles,
May you preserve our health and youth
And hold that steadfast wellspring open
Which spouts forth life and beauty

Frigge

Frige, Frigga, Frijjo

Frigge, the queen of heaven, has a network of symbols
that are quite congruent with Hera's, which is fortunate for us
because the primary sources regarding the goddess are somewhat shallow. Her name has a few possible origins, but is
generally thought to mean "Beloved." We are reminded of the
passage of Plato's *Cratylus* where Socrates conjectures that
Hera's name either derives from the same root as "eros" and
was given to her because of Zeus' desire for her, or that it derives from the word for air and is related to her atmospheric
qualities. Both descriptions suit Frigge, who possesses a blue
cape that symbolizes the skies and a set of falcon plumes.

Frigge rules over marriage and fertility, but is also
heavily associated with prophecy, especially secret prophecy.
Again we are faced with that northern opaqueness, which
with Frigge is also partly manifested in the mediation of her
powers through her twelve handmaidens: Saga, Eir, Gefjon,
Fulla, Sjofn, Lofn, Var, Vor, Syn, Hlin, Snotra, and Gna. These
goddesses are almost analogous to the Muses and Graces but
can also be considered as different "faculties" of Frigge.

Though these goddesses all deserve more detailed treatments and hymnals, which are planned for future editions, their powers must at least be summarized here.

Saga is the goddess of stories, history, narrative, and memory. Hers is a wide and very important subject that I will eventually discuss alongside Mnemosyne and the Muses. Eir is concerned with health, healing, and fate. Gefjon oversees the processes of gifting and generosity and receives women who die unmarried in her hall. Fulla is the sole confidant of Frigge's prophetic secrets, besides for her husband Odin on occasion. Sjofn and Ljofn draw people into loving relationships, with Lofn being specifically concerned with overcoming obstacles to love. Var guarantees oaths and contracts, especially the marriage-oath, another connection to Hera. Vor is all-seeing and is responsible for discerning between what should and should not be kept secret. Syn guards the gate of Frigge's hall and is associated with justice and trials. Hlin is a protector and savior goddess, provider of refuge, and comforter of the mourning. Snotra is the goddess of good manners, civil conduct, and diplomacy. Finally, Gna carries Frigge's messages throughout the many worlds and ferries prayers back to Frigge.

Perhaps the most important and illustrative mythic episode regarding Frigge is in the story of Balder's killing. Frigge, as a devoted mother, was concerned with a prophecy foretelling Balder's death. She went about and demanded an oath from everything in existence that they would not harm him. All complied, but Frigge failed to demand an oath from the mistletoe plant, and so Loki was able to fashion a spear from it and trick the blind god Hodr into throwing it at Baldr, killing him. This killing will be discussed further in baldr's chapter, as well as god-death generally in the Norse corpus, as it's a significant and curious point of departure from most other pagan traditions, including seemingly that of the pre-viking age Germanic peoples.

Eventually Hel revealed that she would release Balder from her realm on the condition that all things in existence wept for him, and so Frigge once again went out to beseech everything in all the worlds. All of them obeyed and wept, especially the mistletoe, but the Gods were thwarted by Loki who, in the guise of a giantess, refused to weep for Baldr. And so Frigge continued to grieve, and Balder would not be released until ragnarok. What is perhaps meant to be communicated by this episode is that the divine wills the return of its descended portions, but cannot secure it without the re-commitment of those portions to unity, which is a decision that may only be made by the divinity that is within them rather than above them.

As made plain by her handmaidens, Frigge's domain is vast and the number of things she may be entreated for are limitless. It is in cases like this that devotees should remember to concern themselves more with the "personality" and the godhead of the deity than with any particular roles or narratives. Honor her by seeing her at work in all of your relationships and the persons involved.

With this in mind, may Mother Frigge now come to hear our prayers and to guide our fates.

Hymn to Mother Frigge

Knowing all and speaking nothing
Save to Fulla's gentle ear,
The queen of Heaven hides all things
Until the time Odin declares

The life that lives in acorns
And in slowly sprouting pine,
That hidden life is yours to hold
And yours to share, in time

When the groom of fruitful earth
Descends in fearsome gales,
Frigge brings the whirling spheres
Forth from under Ymir's veil

Frigge's Love and Piety Prayer

Mother Frigge, Prophetess,
Conjoining all in love,
May you dispel illusion from our mortal eyes
So that we may pursue the highest things in life
With deep affection in our hearts,
Unencumbered by the false,
Harmoniously bonded
With our kin and kith and spirits

Woden and Frigge's Family Prayer

Lord and Lady, Prophesiers, sky-blue Frigge and Woden,
Knowing all and seeing, deftly tugging strings of fate
To ward away all evil and to prosper well the good,
May you look kindly on our house and all of our threads
So that we may remain as one and always in your graces,
Nested safely under gentle Hlin

Poseidon

Neptune, The Earth-Shaker

Poseidon is the midpoint of the Zeus-Poseidon-Plouton triad which is mythologically responsible for the titanomachy, the triumph of the Olympians over the primordial Titans. Their deeds can be compared to the previously discussed slaughter of Ymir, though Kronos was not killed and it is somewhat unclear what exactly differentiated a God from a Titan in the eyes of the ancient Greeks, as several Titanic gods received cultus and Ouranos and Kronos were considered members of another Zeus-trinity.

When the three brothers emerged victorious from the titanomachy, they each took a third of existence for their realm; Zeus the heavens beyond the firmament, Poseidon the waters and midheaven, and Plouton the underworld, with the overworld of Earth (comparable to Midgard) being declared fair game for all of their intervention. It can be said that the three brothers each represent the way that the demiurge manifests himself within the confines of the different levels of existence, growing "colder" and "heavier" the further he emanates from the supreme principle.

There is linguistic and archaeological evidence that Poseidon served as chief god to the Mycenaeans and possibly the Minoans at certain points in their history, as well as being at times conflated with Plouton and Dionysos. Here his association with bulls is important, as the bull is not only a sign of might, vitality, and embodiment, but also has solar connotations in the symbolism of his horns. This solar symbolism would be important to a chief god and is perhaps relevant to the Iliad's account of a battle between Poseidon and Apollo, casting them as a mutually-reinforcing dyad.

Ancient exegetes explained this battle as a naturalistic myth, since ancient physics held that the orb of the sun was fueled by the waters as it passed under the world through Oceanus each night. If we apply that same line of reasoning to spiritual rather than material matters, where it is more warranted, then we may see Poseidon and Apollo as forming a pair through which souls are purified and drawn upwards. The tempted or forgetful soul plunges into the tumultuous rushing waters of creation, seeking to acquire the riches beneath them. In its pursuit, though, the soul is scrubbed clean by the swirling salt and exhausted by swimming, and so learns to look back towards the sun for direction and nourishment.

Neoplatonically, Poseidon joins Zeus and Hephaistos as a world-shaper, presiding over the positive Being that Zeus projects from the supreme principle and overseeing its animation, as water is a nourishing and life-giving element. The association of Poseidon's waters with the fires of the Sun will be relevant again when Hephaistos is discussed.

The waters, when they are calm and favorable to the traveller, become like a mirror cleanly reflecting the light of the sun. That reflection can be helpful to the journeyman, but he can also deceive himself when looking upon it by confusing the sign for the signified. It is when that illusion begins to set in that the waves begin breaking, like stampeding horses, another creature sacred to Poseidon (and further evidence of his identity as at least partially an Indo-European sky father, with pastoralist arrivals to Hellas coming to see the ocean as comparable to the open steppe).

Poseidon is interested in seeing you to your destination, regardless if that destination is where you think it is or where you think you want it to be. Astrologically he is intertwined with the planets of Neptune and Jupiter and the constellation Pisces, which is concerned with altered perception and with exploring one's aquatic interiors and dissolving barriers (the planet Mercury is in its detriment in Pisces because Hermes prefers to unify through connection rather than assimilation).

The devotee may invoke the King of the Seas for anything regarding his or her inner life, destiny, works, and general vitality. The indelible impression of anyone approaching him is one of unstoppable force and weight, which is fearsome if opposed but supremely comforting and encouraging if embraced. Through him obstacles are either washed away or slowly eroded. Honor him by cultivating energetic dedication and partaking in activities that induce the creative or active "flow state."

May the Lord Poseidon now hear our prayers, and may they bring him joy.

Orphic Hymn 17 - Poseidon

Hear, wine-tressed Poseidon,
Holding Earth between your palms,
You wield the trident, God of the stallion,
Dwelling in ocean's full-bosomed foundations

Deep-roaring earth-shaker, ruler of waters,
The waves are like blossoming orchards of flowers
As you rush and drive your horses forth
Across the splashing, frothing brine

You won the third portion, the unfathomed sea,
And grew to love the wild waves
whose creatures praise your godly heart;

Wide-sung God, may you preserve
The earth's deep-buttressed wet foundation
And bring your riches, health and joy,
To us whose vessels course your ocean

Hymn to Poseidon

Who could dare to lift his eyes
Above the fearsome course of waves?
On brazen skin the salt-brine sizzles
Underneath the scorching Sun

Bull of gold, Bull of brass, The shelves of Earth
All quake and grind beneath those hooves
Urged forth by You who drives the waves
With blessed, sceptered, broad command

Lord Poseidon, well of souls, titanic and profound,
Up from untamed waters rise great monsters,
Woe and wealth,
And sacred understanding waits
For those who leave the shore
To travel with Athena, she who steers the wooden walls

Poseidon's Prayer

Poseidon of the waters,
God who sends the rolling waves,
May you with royal power
Spur my soul to greater works,
And, tireless with stallion's might,
Grant us lives so full of life,
Abounding with your blessings

Neptune's Journey Prayer

Gracious God of open ocean,
Neptune, sailors' guide and friend,
May you instruct us always
In what words and acts are pleasing
So that our journeys meet good ends
By your strength and mercy

Njorth

Njord, Njorðr,

Njorth is the god of the sea's bounty, the patriarch of the Vanir, and the father of Ingvi-Frey and the goddess Freya. The life-giving and generative properties of water are exaggerated in him; He himself and both of his children are fertility deities, and it's hypothesized that his name is etymologically related to the proto-Germanic peace and fertility goddess Nerthus. If this connection is warranted, it would mean Njorth's name derives from the Proto-Indo-European *ner-*, meaning "vigorous" or "healthy".

Njorth is married to Skadi, though the myths present the union as uncomfortable. Supposedly Njorth does not want to live at Skadi's mountain home and Skadi does not want to live on the seaside. Their conflict can be said to represent the tension between expansion and restriction, as Skadi is a lawkeeper concerned with boundaries, while their union may be said to represent the codependence of expansion and restriction in order to produce generation.

Early in the marriage the pair attempts to compromise by spending nine days at Skadi's home and three days at Njorth's. This may illustrate how, in the process of creation, one fourth initiates while the remaining three fourths animate, harmonize, and maintain, and that those final three fourths occur once the proverbial mountain has already begun to rise from the primordial waters as it did for Pyrrha and Deucalion.

Njorth is connected to the rune Laguz, ᛚ, the rune of generative water. Laguz is the sub-conscious and pre-conscious life force which is explored and structured by consciousness. "Aquatic" deities such as Njord are those who are at the frontline of that process and so whose barriers become blurred as the mysterious waters give rise to the ecstasy of mystery, discovery, and transformation.

Njorth can be addressed for anything regarding peace, wealth, and creativity. Notably, his worship endured even into the 1800's among isolated Scandinavian fishing communities. Again there is an obvious Piscean connection. The devotee may find him gentle and generous or indifferent and inscrutable, depending on his or her own relationship with the mystery and unpredictability of the deep waters. Honor him by finding peace and joy in productive things like art or work, or, if you are so inclined, start a family.

Father Njorth, may you now hear our prayers and find pleasure in our praises.

Hymn to Njorth

The crashing fires of Muspellheimr
Thrashed against the stagnant ice;
Glaciers bled, their boiling tears
Are now your happy waters

Heat and freedom ride the seas
As waves that twist and rise,
With heaving breaths your sky-wide chest
Sends fortune to your praisers

Warlike Freya, peaceful Ing,
Your blessed son and daughter,
For all the joys they bring to man,
Threefold we hail Njorth, their father

Njorth's Prayer for Wealth

Coursing God, seafaring Njorth,
Keeper of the ocean's treasures,
May you reward our works with riches
And drive away all ruinous waves

Njorth's Fertility Prayer

Vanatyr, great father God,
Sire of blameless Ing and Freya,
If ever I offer drink to you
Or sing your name with glee,
May you share with me the joy
Of waxing pride in my own issue,
Of lovely sons and daughters
Who may grace my home with spotless health

Demeter

Ceres, Thesmophoros

Demeter is the mother goddess par excellence, especially as regards agricultural society. She individuates and elaborates Life into the plurality of lives that participate in it, reminiscent of how a wheat field hosts many ears of grain and an ear of grain many kernels. She is also the power by which lives are self-generative, renewing themselves through union rather than requiring continuous re-constitution from above. Thus where Njorth, Zeus, etc. may be considered to provide "monadic," emanating, paternal, or self-total fertility, Demeter furnishes the cosmos with dyadic, maternal, or mutually-contingent fertility.

As with Poseidon and Zeus, Demeter can be seen as projecting powers shared by Hera into progressive levels of emanation, especially as regards her connection with law. The ancients viewed the laws of civilization and culture as natural extensions of the laws that govern nature and the crop cycle, and so of course the Goddess of one would be the Goddess of the other as well. In fact the Polis itself, the unit of civilization, was likened to a cultivated field juxtaposed against the savage hinterlands called "Utgard" by the Norse.

The entwinement of culture with agri-culture continues today, though diluted by industrial farming. These concepts also share a root with the religious terms "cult" and "cultus." Agriculture cultivates and makes useful the Earth, Culture cultivates, focuses, and beautifies the human mind and living-space, and Cultus cultivates the connection of the human soul to its divine origin. As the Thesmophoros, "Lawbringer," Demeter stands at the junctions of all of these things to nurture and proliferate them, bringing the rules and tools that trim and train our growth to coax it into its most beautiful form.

Mythologically Demeter is most prominently featured in the story of Persephone's capture and marriage to Pluto, which is the centerpiece of the Eleusinian mystery. Here she is the grieving mother, reminiscent of Frigge. In protest of the marriage, she makes the earth barren and deprives mankind of all plant life, forcing Zeus to acquiesce out of pity for humans. When Persephone is allowed to return to the overworld for a portion of the year, Demeter rejoices and returns fertility to the earth, beginning the growing season. Beyond the obvious natural allegory, this cycle is meant to remind us of the immortality of the soul, which manifests itself in the world of change not as something unchanging but as something that is constantly renewing. As the Gita says, "Death is certain for one who has been born, and rebirth is inevitable for one who has died."

In the context of the myth's narrative, Demeter's actions may also represent the human emotional attachment to the world of generation, which is necessarily the world of decay. It is significant that in her grief she abdicates her throne in heaven, descending to Earth to wander in search of her daughter. In her absence from heaven and her absorption in the world, the world suffers barrenness in order to reveal that the generative principle, the cause of birth and life and flowering, must be beyond the material despite infusing and inhabiting material things. The proper state of things is only restored, the material world only made fruitful and divinely sanctioned again, when the fallen Demeter finally looks upon Persephone, the soul, reuniting with her and reassuming her throne on Olympus.

Demeter should be thanked and approached for matters involving food and diet, agriculture, wealth and bounty (especially in the family or community), social harmony, grief, and coping with change. Honor her with gratitude for your meals and for the turning of the season, especially if you are celebrating with family and friends or are involved in farming or gardening.

Great Mother Demeter, may you now come to hear our prayers and give us comfort.

Orphic Hymn 40 - Eleusinian Demeter

Divine mother goddess of all that exists,
Many-named Demeter, nourishing youths,
Giver of wealth, by you we prosper,
Who nurtures the delicate ears of grain

Giver of wealth and rejoicer in labor,
Delighted by peace when your worshippers gather
To sow and to thresh and to heap in your honor
The ripening fruits that you dwell in, unfettered

In Eleusis' sacred valley you dwell,
Charming, lovely, all-sustaining,
You who was first to yoke the ox
And gush from black soil the rich, blessed harvest

You are growth and blooming life,
You shining friend of Bromios,
Torch-bearing pure one, delighting in summer,
The fruit of the sickle is yours to bring

Yoking your car to the rich-gleaming dragons,
Whirling and howling around your bright throne,
You are the mother of earth and of mortals,
Ecstatic in wide-reaching breadth of your works

All the many tribes of flowers,
Grains and beasts and vegetables,
Tell us the secrets of ten thousand faces,
A blossom for each of your myriad powers

May you come, blessed Goddess, holy Demeter,
Come bearing the fruits of your bright timeless summer,
Bringing peace, law, and riches with prosperous honors
And come to bring wide-brimming health to us all

Demeter's Prayer

Mother Demeter, Persephone's warden,
Withhold not your bounty from mortals,
But happily grant us the means of good living,
Shroud us in wisdom and hold our hearts near
To drive away danger and strip us of fear

Sif

The Golden-Haired

Sif, the wife of Thor, is the goddess of agriculture, and specifically of the harvest and the harvesting season. By some accounts she is the mother of the winter-god Ullr. Her primary attribute is a head of magnificently shining long blond hair, representing mature wheat. It is said that Loki, who is perhaps a sort of Promethean figure, once cut her hair. For this crime, he is forced by the Aesir to replace the hair, which he does by charging dwarves to craft a wig made of strands of pure gold that flow and grow just like real hair. This may be meant to indicate how man's artifice can damage the earth but is also capable of making it fruitful and useful, even moreso than before.

Sif is connected to the rune Jera, ᛃ. This rune concerns the harvest months and the karmic, cyclical path of the sun through the wheel of the year. It is the rune of union between Heaven and Earth, with the seasons serving as periods of drama in their marriage - separation in winter, intimacy in summer, and transition in spring and fall. It is the rune of the fruits of action, planning, and cultivation, the rune of agri-*cultural* Demetrian law.

Unfortunately there is little surviving information from primary sources on this goddess, but her association with Ullr and with Thor may indicate an elevated importance to pre-viking era Germanic peoples. She is described congruently with other "Earth Mother" deities and may be approached for the same reasons as any of them, such as fertility, nourishment, hospitality, and growth. Honor her by gardening or by undertaking any endeavor that you know will take patience to bear fruit.

May lady Sif now attend to these prayers, and regard her praisers with kindness and generosity.

Hymn to Sif

Rolling rainclouds, rolling fields
Echo with your praise,
Rolling waves of summer winds
Whistle through your golden grain

Restless spirits burgeon through you,
Restless spirits bloom,
Bursting through the blue-dark soil
Taking up the shifting form

And when the amber sun at dusk
Shimmers on the ruddy scythe,
Mother Sif with gentle steps
Will gather up the sheaves

Sif's Prayer

Hail, Goddess, spouse of Thor,
Golden Sif who tends the grain,
If ever we have pleased you
Then may steady work be duly paid
And our house's bounty piled high

Plouton

Pluto, Dis Pater, the Hidden One

The Lord of the Dead is known to most by a more common name, one which for the ancients was taboo to speak for fear of invoking his attention incautiously or at inopportune moments. Though you are free to use his popular name, it is my preference to keep the tradition because, in my opinion, it lends to the awe and mystique of the God. It is considered luckier or more appropriate to address him as Pluto or Plouton, as this name refers to his rich bounty of ores and gems rather than to his more grim roles.

Plouton is one of the three sons of Saturn. He is actually eldest of them, being born before Poseidon and Zeus. This may be in order to represent that his realm, being farthest from heaven, has been separated from it for the "longest". Plouton is called the "all-receiver," for just as everything originates in Zeus it eventually arrives in Plouton's hands. The two gods, or faces of the demiurge, form poles between which life and generation play out, and yet Plouton as Zeus Chthonios reminds us that this drama is never truly separate from or outside of its source. Plouton reminds us of the presence of divinity even at the furthest extremities of existence, extremities where he occupies himself with the purification of souls who have made their way so far from their origin.

Amusingly, Plato in the *Cratylus* describes Plouton not as a dread prison warden but as an eminent philosopher, with the following reasoning: Desire compels people's behavior much more strongly than punitive authority does, and so in order to keep the souls of the dead from drifting out of his realm Plouton must make them desire being there. He does this by providing to them the greatest object of desire for the soul, knowledge. Thus he is called the Rich One on account of his wealth of knowledge, and called the Hidden One on account of the fact that he is not revealed until the garments of matter are cast off.

Astrologically this god is intertwined with, of course, Pluto and the constellation Scorpio, whose purifying and resurrecting power he shares with Herakles and Dionysos. Pluto girds the outer limit of this solar system and has the slowest orbital speed, allowing it to serve as a sort of consistent baseline for the astrological drama occuring over generations.

Plouton may be (carefully and gravely) approached for matters regarding mourning, money, the darker or more hidden parts of life, the pursuit of knowledge, contracts, and preparation of oneself for the final journey. His marriage to Persephone is also of importance, being a theogamia like Zeus and Hera's. By some accounts the pair looks kindly on happy marriages and allows them to continue after death. Being the preeminent Chthonic deity, it is of course appropriate to treat him as such in ritual by holding one's hands palm-down and burying or burning (rather than consuming) offerings to him.

Having thus spoken of you, may the rich father Plouton come to hear our prayers and reward our praises.

Orphic Hymn 18 - Plouton

Plouton, most generous, whose most profound domain
Dwells beneath the silent earth, the firm unyielding earth,
In Tartarean meadows thickly wrapped in deepest shade

Terrestrial Zeus, Sceptered Zeus Chthonios,
May you accept this offering, O Plouton,
You who holds the keys to open all the depths of earth

The wealth of earth, the wealth of years, the wealth of fruits
By you is given, you who rules that lap of mortals,
Shifting Earth, the queen of All

A windless, distant, tireless place
Does host your throne's abode
Above the gloomy Acheron that girds the roots of worlds

All-receiver, mortals' master, host of endless masses,
You who took to be your bride Demeter's purest daughter
Tore her from her meadow flying through the sea in rapture

Impelled by love, upon dark steeds
You flew across the deep until
The blessed gates of Eleusis rose up to meet your gaze

You alone were born to judge the secret deeds of mortals,
Holy ruler over all, delighting in our reverence,
May you come with favor and with joy to hear our prayers

Hymn to Pluto

You, who walks freely
Between the many silences lodged in every stone,
Gathering up the dead with hands
As cold as aquifers,
To cleanse the heads of passers-by.

Fresh earth, and shining gems, and virgin ores, and You,
Are the long blink of a pious eye
Returning to the Highest
Through all His lovely worlds

Plouton's Prayer

Great father, rich father, bountiful Dis Pater,
Giver of great riches and of wisdom,
May you safeguard my house the means of fullest living,
And ensure that we are pure and whole
Whenever we must go to you

Persephone

Proserpina, Kore

Persephone, the Queen of the Underworld, is the centerpiece of the Eleusinian mysteries. She is the personality to which initiates anchor themselves, participating in her drama as a part of her. In this capacity she can be compared to Dionysos in his own mysteries. Where Dionysos furnishes the human soul with its "God-ness," its monadic procession, Persephone furnishes its "Goddess-ness," its dyadic fertility. Where Dionysos leads us through destruction in order to reveal what is indestructible, Persephone illumines the presence of immortality within the recurring cycle of generation and destruction itself.

Herself an arbiter of change and fluctuation, Kore is wed to the steely, unshifting Plouton who is her anchor. This union serves to show that generation, growth, emanation, has a lower limit before it dissipates that is buttressed by Chthonic Zeus who contains all that he himself, as Ouranic Zeus, generates.

When Kore is reunited with her mother, it may be meant to show that the parental care of the Gods for their creation prohibits a soul from being permanently locked in the stillness of the underworld, perhaps because energy cannot be destroyed or created but only transformed. Nonetheless Persephone must return to her husband each year because before she was released she was tricked into eating pomegranate seeds.

The pomegranate is a symbol of fertility and multiplicity, having such an abundance of sweet seeds. Here it is meant to indicate that the soul is drawn downwards and bound to the world of change when it takes multiplicity and generation for goods in themselves rather than as the fruits of a higher providence, the form of the Good. By eating the seeds the soul is destined to follow their path, a path which leads to the embrace of Plouton whose wisdom and purification enables the following ascent back into the light.

Kore should be thanked and evoked in matters of change and transformation, personal growth, grief, and distressing long-term situations. Above all, she reminds us to remain tender, attentive, and hopeful through the trials of life. As a Chthonic goddess, guidelines applying to Plouton are also relevant to her.

Great Kore, may you now incline to our prayers and bless them with your generosity.

Orphic Hymn 29 - Persephone

Persephone, O Blessed daughter, Only daughter
Of highest Zeus and great Demeter,
Come to witness and accept
This, our grateful sacrifice

Honored spouse of Pluto,
Vivifying and discreet,
Commanding dreadful gates
Within the bowels of the earth

Golden-tressed avenging Goddess,
Purest bloom of lady De,
You mother of the Furies
Who came forth from hidden bonds

Mother of the Counselor
Who roars with many shapes,
You, radiant and luminous,
Who dances with the seasons

Revered and mighty virgin,
Shining, horned, and rich in fruits,
Sole-beloved of mortals
Who finds joy in meadows' breeze

When, in spring, you show yourself,
Your figure, holy and sublime
Teems in branches green with fruits
Until the fall brings Pluto's car

You alone are life and death
To ever-toiling mortals,
Persephone, you nourish all
And reap when reaping's due

Hear us, blessed goddess,
And send forth the deep earth's fruits
As you blossom, green with peace
And firm in gentle health

O Kore, bring a blameless life
And splendor in the waxing years
Of he who sails to your realm,
To mighty Pluto's kingdom

Hymn to Kore

Peer of Zeus in counsel, blameless Kore, blessed queen,
How could any mortal eye behold your timeless bloom
And fail to be fastened tight to vast and sacred stillness?

Euboulaia, suffer not to see your children
Bound and broke on shifting wheels,
Chewing sand with bleeding gums

But come, instead, with all your wisdom
Abreast the winds of fearful change
To still the hearts of childish men

For Deo wept and Dias grinned
When in the sacred plains you clasped
The hands of Pluto, saying "Hark!"

"A virgin goes to rule the dead,
No grieving cries will raise her,
No river stills its dreadful eddy, such is Tethys' will;

But I, the one who witnesses, who goes now to be seen,
Will freely cross Eleusis' gates, as mother and as bride
To show that noone perishes
Who comes to know the Seer"

Kore's Prayer

Divine Kore, maiden and bride,
May you come in times of change
To teach a mortal what is changeless,
May you teach a fleeting heart to fix itself on the most high,
And, when this is accompished,
May it bring us wealth and life

Dionysos

Bacchus, Liber, Zagreus

Dionysos, the liberator, the conqueror, the son of Zeus, is the ruler of the incarnate world and the sub-lunar face of the demiurge. He is the god of mystery and of the destruction of illusion, a process that is always jarring and usually involves delving further into altered mindsets. Thus Dionysos presides over intoxication and is the giver of wine, which undergoes its own katabasis in its creation - the grapes are trod on and placed underground to ferment, emerging more powerful and more distilled than they had been before. There are many myths about Dionysos, too many to recount here. The one we will discuss is his birth as Zagreus, dismemberment by titans, and rebirth as Dionysos, which is important to the Orphic theology.

It was said that Persephone bore a son of Zeus, which he named Zagreus, "great hunter". He was so pleased and impressed with the child that he sat him on his throne and gave him the thunderbolt, declaring the child his co-ruler and heir. Zagreus, because of his newfound power, was coveted by a troop of titans, representative of the lower world. These titans lured the child away from his throne and thunderbolts by enticing him with a basket full of seven toys: A golden apple representing immortality, a pinecone representing creative force and endurance, a ball representing the sphere of the cosmos, a spinning top which represents the cyclical, entropic swirl of time, A tuft of hair signifying growth and wildness, knuckle-bone dice signifying boyhood and playfulness as well as fate and chance, and finally a mirror said to be crafted by Hephaistos. This last is the most important of the toys.

The infant Zagreus was fascinated by the mirror, and while he was distracted looking at himself the Titans snatched him. Zagreus is dismembered, cooked, and eaten by the titans, with the exception of his heart and his limbs. Proclus speaks of this:

> "A mirror was a symbol of... the intellectual completion of the universe. Hence they say, Vulcan (Ἡφαιστος) made a mirror for Dionysus, into which the God looking, and beholding the image of himself, proceeded into the whole partible fabrication of things."

That is to say that Dionysus, as an instantiation of the Demiurge and therefore a noetic being, produces the world by witnessing and contemplating himself as both subject and object.

The moment at which Zagreus perceives himself in the mirror, the moment at which the titans snatch him, is the moment at which he descends into the incarnate realm to become its master, as the incarnate realm is a fountain-like overflow of divine self-witnessing through which lower beings in turn perceive the divine.

He is said to be "torn apart" in this process because this world, as described earlier in regards to Discordia and the golden apple, is formed out of tension between opposites, the first of these opposites being the bifurcation between subject and object which occurs when Zagreus peers into the mirror.

Smelling the smoke of the titans' fire, Zeus sends Athena and Apollo. Apollo saves the limbs of Zagreus while Athena rescues his still-beating heart and returns it to Zeus. Here the heart is emblematic of the soul as a thing that endures through many forms, worlds, and incarnations, as when Dionysos is re-constituted he will no longer "be" Zagreus but will still carry his soul. Apollo, the purifier, takes the limbs of Zagreus because they are emblematic of the material parts that do not survive reincarnation.

Zeus soon fell in love with Semele, a princess of Thebes and the daughter of Harmonia, child of Ares and Aphrodite. She was impregnated with the heart of Zagreus, but Hera tricked her into demanding that Zeus show her his true form. Zeus, because he had previously promised Semele anything she desired, was forced to keep his word when she made her request. When he shone on her with the full force of a God, Semele was burned up and annihilated. The grieving Zeus retrieved Dionysos from her womb and sewed him up in his thigh (perhaps a euphemism for loins, though both convey the symbolic meaning of vitality and strength). Thus Dionysos was thrice-born, once from the goddess Kore, once from the mortal Semele, and once from Zeus alone.

Semele demonstrates both the possibility of intimacy with divine reality and the inaccessibility of that reality's infinite entirety to a human's bodily mind. It is worth clarifying that Semele's fate was actually not intended to be taken as a negative thing. Tragic, yes, but a tragedy in the service of evoking a genuine religious sentiment. Her death is an apotheosis, the pinnacle of what is possible to human souls, a fate much preferable to slow decay in the Greek imagination.

Semele was of great importance to the Dionysian cult, which in large part was actually a cult of motherhood. The maenads, the wild revelers of his retinue, supposedly suckled the cubs of wild beasts and strangers' children at their breasts. Dionysos is the divine child who dissolves barriers, including the barrier between his earthly mothers and the gods.

It is clear that wine, with its process of fermentation and its ability to intoxicate, is the perfect symbol and product of the God. The elements of release, honesty, frenzy, free flow, and also terror and danger, teach us much about him. The reflective surface of the wine is Zagreus' mirror. Dionysos heightens & sharpens our experience of the physical world because he wants us to confront and surpass it. As a God he is actually closer to an ascetic than a hedonist; all that he does and moves in us is towards the ends of peace and freedom from discursive fear and desire.

Through his dismemberment and rebirth, through his choosing to descend the ladder of creation to reveal himself, we are reminded that we are nothing less or more than indestructible souls. Once Dionysos, from his throne atop this world, succeeds in teaching us this, we become able to approach the throne of Zeus upon Olympus, which aims to return our souls to our Gods just as Dionysos returns our conscious focus and experience to our souls.

The separator, the liberator, the conqueror, is not a patient God. He is irrepressable, undeniable, and already tirelessly at work in your life whether you recognize him or not. At every moment when you encounter something uncanny, something beyond yourself, something that strikes you and forces you to commit yourself fully to an experience, that is the God reaching through the mirror to grab you by the collar and pull you as close as you will let him. At every point at which your life changes forever, at which you slide between entire modes of being, that is Dionysos pouring you a new cup and reminding you of one thing: Your body, your environment, your people, even your mind, these are all extensions of you but they are not your entirety. You are not the seven toys, you are not the reflection in the mirror, you are the child.

Dionysos is intertwined with Aphrodite. Love requires recognition, a clear vision of the Other. Aphrodite furnishes us with desire and love for the Other in service of her harmonizing mission. Meanwhile Dionysos, as the great revealer, helps us to recognize our true selves within the Other, selves whose division and alienation from each other is actually ultimately temporary and illusory. Dionysian Love is the self-love of an egoless self sprawling itself out to its true size, encompassing all around it like the explosive shoots of ivy that sprout wherever the God steps.

It was those shoots of ivy that destroyed his prison in Thebes and overthrew the rapacious pirates that threatened him on his journey westward. The irrepressible bloom of life is the God's weapon, a weapon wielded in service of the recognition of non-duality, a challenge issued to the devotee: "I dare you to look at the twisting, splitting, writhing tangle of vines and to see only Me, situated within and beyond them, unmoving and all-pervading like the heat of a fire."

Dionysos, like his father, may be addressed and thanked for nearly anything. You may find him almost more present in experiences than in worship, and so it is fitting to turn your experiences into worship and your worship into an experience. You may find he often comes unexpectedly; this is simply his nature and should be embraced.

Father Dionysos, may you now bear witness to our prayers and praises, and may they be pleasing to you.

Orphic Hymn 30 - Dionysos

I call to Dionysos, roaring loud in revelry,
First born, doubled, thrice incarnate, raging Bacchic Lord,
Ineffable and secretive, savage, double-natured,
Wearing mighty rutting horns

Wrapped in ivy, warlike bull, howling with divinity,
Receiving beasts' raw flesh at feasts,
Wrapped in vines and decked in grapes

Eubouleus, Counselor, of Zeus and Kore born,
When they were joined in secret bonds;
May you, O deathless, happy mind
Gladly hear my voice and breathe
With gentle sweetness on my prayers,
You, with all your nurses

Orphic Hymn 45 - Dionysos Bassareus

Holy Dionysos, come,
You bull-faced fiery God,
Bassareus, Bacchus,
Master over all, you God
Who wears so many names

You delight in dripping swords
And in the comfort of the maenads,
You howl through Olympos
Frenzied Bacchus, Roaring One

Armed with pine-tipped thyrsus
And with high exceeding wrath,
You are honored utterly
By all among both Gods and men
Who dwell on your soft earth

Come, great Dionysos,
You happy leaping God,
And bring forth in your retinue
Abundant joy for all

Hymn to Silvan Dionysos

You! You who presses grapes, O Roaring God, you
Of foaming mouth, exceeding praise
For you our joy
Must spill in waves from too-full cups

Praise like sap of Maple,
Praise like Thunder striking Oak,
Praise like bursting cones of Pine
We praise you, thrice-born fruit of vine

You thunder-tongued God who wields
The fruit-tipped scepter, Phoeban bolts
Gather in praise around your hair,
Where melting snow is sunshine's mirror

Praise like gushing honeycomb,
Praise like rushing avalanche,
Praise like armor rattling loose,
We praise you, thrice-born son of Zeus

Hymn to Liber Pater

Raving God, you tore the yoke and shackle,
Shattered Theban bonds
And rent their king from limb to limb like tender veal

The push and the pull of the undulant wine,
Your shivering ivy arms
Strike and awaken the minds of mortals
Lusting after shadows

Raging One, you shred the muscled veil,
Mighty teeth and hands
Abound in savage strength against
Mankind's most bitter blindness

Holy Dionysos, You arrive without a warning
To perform your holy works,
And through you all things go to join the God of Gods

Dionysos' Prayer

Gentle Dionysos, master of the blooming world,
As everything incarnate blossoms forth from your great love
And from the vast almighty heart of Zeus,
So may you fashion my own in this image,
So that I might share in your act of creation,
Unbounded by all thoughts of lack

Dionysos' Inspiration Prayer

Princely Dionysos, freely flowing, unencumbered,
Please grant my mind a peace and freedom
Fit to follow yours,
Fit to hear the heavens' birdsong,
Fit to sing your hymns aloud

Dionysos' Liberation Prayer

Dionysos, dancing god, carefree Lord of all,
May you loosen all the ropes and chains
That bind me to my worldly fears
And gently lead me into bliss
And peaceful union with the Gods

Ingvi-Frey

Freyr, Ing, the Lord of Peace

Ingvi-Frey, the son of Njorth and twin of Freya, is the provider of peace and plenty, and more precisely of the freedom and sovereignty that comes from these things. He is associated with fertility, sacral kingship, horses, and revelry. Frey tirelessly makes manifest the drive of the divine to fashion its descendents in its own image, encouraging peace, freedom, and wealth as the closest earthly approximations of the state of unity and superabundance which the gods embody. These gifts can be taken quite literally, but only if it is also understood that behind them and supporting them lie inner peace, freedom from spiritual encumbrance, and the wealth of wisdom and virtue.

Frey's most prominent myth is his courtship of the giantess Gerd. One day, while Odin is away, Frey sits on Odin's throne Hlidskjálf and looks out upon the whole of the nine worlds. In Jotunheim he sees a beautiful girl, the etin Gerd, in the house of her father Gymir whose homestead is encircled with flame. Gerd's limbs are so radiant that they light up the sea and the sky, and Frey becomes lovesick and does not

132

speak or eat for days. Eventually he is goaded into revealing his predicament to his squire Skirnir. Skirnir offers to travel to jotunheim to win Gerd's hand in marriage for Frey, and for the rest of the myth he acts as the god's representative.

Before continuing, we will note the meanings of some names: Gerd means "the fenced-in one" and Skirnir means "bright one." Gerd as a jotun is associated with the lower world, and Skirnir is tasked with uniting her to a God. To accomplish his mission, Frey gives Skirnir a horse which can pass through fire and his magical sword, which famously fights autonomously if its wielder is wise.

When Skirnir finally reaches the house of Gymir, he leaps his horse over the wall of fire and is met by Gerd with suspicion. He explains that he is here to win her over on behalf of Frey, and offers her golden apples of immortality and the self-replicating golden ring Draupnir as gifts. She refuses, as she is very comfortable in her rich father's home. Skirnir changes his tone, brandishing the magic sword and threatening to curse her. The curses include being married to a three-headed ice troll, being imprisoned in a dark place, and being seen by all creatures but not seeing them. At this, Gerd relents, and agrees to meet Frey in nine days. The meeting goes well and they are soon married.

This myth is usually explained as an allegory for the coming of spring, which is inevitable no matter how cold or dark the winter gets. It may also be describing one way for the process of turning towards the gods to play out. Gerd is fenced in, just as humans are fenced in within Midgard, with nothing coming or going from her father's house. When an agent of the divine finally comes, she is suspicious, and refuses his treasures. She believes the worldly treasures of her

house are adequate, even compared to the immortality symbolized by the apples and the fertility symbolized by Draupnir. If the gifts are desirable to her, then they are at least not
desirable enough that she is willing to give up her perceived
independence (despite being her father's ward). She fears
Frey and the change he might bring.

When Skirnir, the bright one, begins to threaten her,
the unseemly display reveals three things. Firstly, that divine
plans, though they are anchored in love, do not require our
agreement in order to continue unfolding. It can be a hand
held out to us, yes, but just as often it can be an ocean current
which it is up to us to follow or be swallowed by. Secondly,
Skirnir outlines not necessarily the intentional punishment
but rather the natural karmic fate of the soul that turns away
from the divine. Instead of being wed to the fruitful god
Frey and participating in his continued creation, one weds
the three-headed frost troll who represents distance from
unity, warmth, and civility. One becomes imprisoned in a
dark place, beheld by all but beholding none, because matter
itself has no light and no positive existence outside of what
is imposed on it by the forms and by souls, and thus to turn
towards the matter rather than towards the forms and souls
animating it leads to darkness. Gerd is swayed by threats
rather than bribes for the same reason that Dionysos comes
suddenly and terribly. The basest forms of the faculties of
desire and aversion, though they should eventually be overcome, can at least be made equally useful to the spiritual
journey until then.

Finally, we are taught the use of Frey's sword, which is
akin to the Buddhist "sword of discrimination." The sword,
a special enemy of beastly jotnar, "fights by itself if its owner
be wise" because the wise mind is always discriminating and

discerning the differences between things in order to ascertain the truth. When Skirnir threatens Gerd with it, he is announcing the conclusions of philosophy which are gained by that sword.

Frey's gift of the sword to Skirnir is permanent, and Frey thereafter lacks it, a circumstance that leads to his fall at Ragnarok. This is to show that once the soul, Gerd, is reunited with its divine origin the sword falls out of use because there is nothing left to be gained and learned by discernment. The loss of Frey's sword is also symbolic of the irrationality of love and the sacrifice of energy and power on the part of the male in order to make the female fruitful.

Frey's rune is Ingwaz, ᛜ, which represents the replenishment of spent power. His strength is held inwardly, gestated, in winter months or times of spiritual sparsity in order to explode out into the world more magnificently in spring. The god is described as blameless and beloved, never causing any distress except by his absence. Those periods of absence, though, are part of his work of furnishing the world with good things, gifts which would not be appreciated without banes to compare them to. We should remember the drama of the Jera rune spoken of in relation to Sif.

Ingvi-Frey should be thanked and besought for matters involving abundance, marriage, fertility, independence, and simple joy. He is eminently pleasant and generous. Honor him by emulating these things as best you can.

Great god Frey, may you now incline to our prayers, and may you receive our thanks, praises, and pleas most graciously.

Hymn to Lord Ing

The golden-bristled boar goes forth to light the path of peace,
Gullinbursti fast erupts to trample down the writhing weeds,
Planting seeds of grain
Wherever dirt is thrown up by his hooves

Father Ing, beloved Frey, you wield ever-blooming peace
In proof that Kingship rests as much
On plowshares as on swords,
For mankind masters both with hopes of freedom

Freedom from the sting of lack,
Freedom from the ache of want,
For man sinks deeper into bondage
When he spurns your gifts,
But you are always present when we learn to call in praise

Hymn to Frey

Wielding the sword, the wand of sharp runes,
You open the ice-coated slow-sobbing Earth,
Heaving, recoiling at fiery touch

Spring, irrepressible, Summer, unbreakable,
Autumn, unflinching, when spear-tips are buried,
And Winter, when mead drips on unfeeling rime

Wielding the antler and words of fleet power,
Surrender the sword into Gerd's dark enclosure,
Let no heart fear the blameless Lord

Bless the green fields and straws beneath lovers,
Bless the bright groves where men's children play,
Bless the glad tongues that sing all your praises,
And bless these words, O Father Frey

Ingvi-Frey's Prayer for Wealth

Father Frey, Abundant God, gushing forth your blessings,
May you make us fruitful with increasing wealth in all things,
And teach us with your sovereign mind
To cherish and to rightly use your gifts

Ingvi-Frey's Peace Prayer

Father Ingvi, great ancestor, raiser of the grain,
Peace and freedom you have pledged
To those who love your many names,
Those who long to draw you near,
And who uphold your works and laws.

May you help us in this endeavor,
Help us to win a sovereign peace,
And always come to hear our prayers
Ingvi-Frey, beloved God

Thor

Thunar, Donar, Bjorn

Thor, the son of Odin, is the bringer of storms and rains and the master of Midgard, enforcing its boundary against the etins and beasts of Utgard. Thor is central to the Aesir, providing both protection with his hammer and wealth with his rains. There is evidence to suggest that to the ancient Germanic peoples he occupied the primary place of honor in the minds of common folk - Odin's cult seems to have been esoteric and mostly partaken in by the upper classes.

Thor is proudly and pointedly un-esoteric, and all the more powerful for it. His role is to nurture good things and destroy bad things, keeping the earth clean so that his wife Sif's work is unencumbered, and he seems to enjoy it. His rune is Thurisaz, Þ, which unlike most runes actually survived lexigraphically as the letter thorn, Þ. It is fitting that the glyph of such a widely-renowned and reluctantly-abandoned god remained present even in the latin alphabet adopted after conversion.

This rune is apotropaic and almost "homeopathic." Thor's opposition to the jotnar works in part because he himself is half-etin, born to the giantess Jord (Eorð, literally Earth). Thurisaz assimilates opposites and projects them outwards with instinctual force. Among those opposites are the fighter and his foe, the defender and the intruder, whose battles create and reveal new powers.

Thor's thunder splits the raincloud, releasing the rains that make crops and wild plants grow. It could be said that the rain is produced by the opposition of Thor's hammer to its victim, usually a jotun. Thus there is a sort of trinity in Thor which is depicted in the points of his rune: the striker above, the stricken below, and in the middle the boon which is won for Sif or for mankind. That boon is both safety and the ability to secure it, both fertility and the power to secure it, as a God effortlessly encapsulates the cause and the result within himself. Thor *is* the fence around Midgard as well as the power that furnishes Midgard's generation, just as a rose is both its thorn and its flower.

The most illustrative of Thor's myths is his enmity with Jormungandr, the world-serpent who encircles the ocean around Midgard. Jormungandr, an example of an Ourobouros, represents the "negative" aspects of the barrier around Midgard, acting as an inhibitor to the natural tendency of the divine to carelessly grow and expand. Certainly Thor himself has such a tendency. Thor forms the barrier by pressing outward, Jormungandr by pressing inward. Their mutual necessity is symbolized by the tale that they destroy each other at Ragnarok. Thor survives long enough after his victory to travel nine paces, nine being the number of ending cycles and transition between realities.

Thor should be thanked and addressed for matters involving protection, victory, willpower, and instinctive, thumotic action. In some ways he is the divine within the worldly, inhabiting it in order to marshall it upwards, akin to the root, sacral, and solar plexus wheels. He is energetic, strenuous, maximalist, straightforward, and jovial, and he fosters these qualities in worshippers. Honor him by embracing these things, by valuing strength and bravery, and by directing libidinal force towards good ends rather than repressing or squandering it.

And so, thundering Lord Thor, may you now come to share our prayers and be pleased by them.

Hymn to Pandemian Thor

You cast out giants' mischief,
O Thunder's Master, Odin's Son,
With pure and potent fury
Do you strike down the vicious ones

You hold your hammer over fields
And all folks' humble homes,
You gladly drink the offered mead
And shatter evil's bones

Your galavanting chariot
Tears across the greying sky,
And we are always joyed to hear
Your laughter roll across Sif's thighs

Thornsong

Thorns are throbbing pain to woman
And frustration unyielding
To man, withstanding and wielding

Ice gathers heat beyond the garth,
The son of Woden sends the storm
In azure tongues to our delight

The rousing strike and soft release
Of Thunder's happy carpentry
Thwarts the trouble giants bring

Thor's Purification Prayer

Loudly-crashing Thor, Midgard's happy warden,
May you who brings your might to bear
Against the backs of vile giants
Drive away all wicked things and spirits
And cleanse our homes and bodies
In the eyes of all the Gods

Thor's Victory Prayer

Father Thor, astride the goats,
The gnashing-goats, relentless,
Bring the rains of bounty
And the weapon that can win them,
Bring the winds by which our kin
May win great heaps of glory

Herakles

Hercules, the Man-God

Herakles, the son of Zeus and the mortal Alcmene, is the pinnacle of mankind and represents what man becomes when he is fully reunited with his divine source, assimilating totally to godhead and mantling it for himself. He has also left us with a mythos which details the process of that ascension. Herakles is the great ancestor-hero who first made the wild earth habitable for man, destroying monsters, founding cities, and leaving behind many descendants.

Herakles is the fruition of the Absolute within the human, a fruition that is only realized after struggle. Herakles' 12 labors each correlate to a segment of the zodiac. Unfortunately the order of the labors has been jumbled in transmission, but it is clear that they begin with the slaying of the Nemean Lion. This is Herakles' initiation as a warrior, corresponding to a widespread prehistoric lion-slaying ritual - Herakles is actually a quite primordial figure, calling back to the very earliest periods of human settlement. His use of a club and bow rather than a sword is testament to this.

The slaying of the Nemean Lion corresponds to the constellation Leo, which is the traditional seat of the Sun, the symbol of sovereignty, vision, and selfhood. From that point on, having attained his full human selfhood, Herakles travels through the karmic wheel whose challenges strengthen and purify him until he overcomes it, moving beyond cause and effect into the world of pure Being. There he is finally deemed worthy by Hera, who was responsible for the bulk of his ill fortune, and is actually his namesake; Hera-Kleos, "Glory of Hera". He then marries her daughter Hebe, the goddess of youth. She represents the liberation of the experiential mind from the ravages of time and decay when it manages to reach the soul which animates its body, fully embracing and experiencing the immortality which it possesses.

When Alexander the Great brought the Hellenistic world into contact with India, the Greek explorer Megasthenes soon encountered worship of Krishna by the tribe of the Shurasenas. After inquiring further about the God and learning of his troubled and prophesied childhood and his slaying of a great serpent, Megasthenes determined that he was analogous to Herakles. Certainly Krishna's supreme immanence, presence, and accessibility lend themselves to comparison, and deep investigation of Herakles will reveal a similar path to the Supreme Principle for the devotee.

Herakles is a god of strength, endurance, perseverance, and the success they bring. Like Thor he is protective and destructive of intruders, and as a very immanent God he is concerned with all matters of the body and the physical world, like health, exercise, and fertility. There are many historical records of Herakles being invoked for healing, especially among the Romans with whom his cult was very popular, and alongside Hermes he is said to be the inventor

of wrestling and the patron of gymnasia. In fact Herakles
presides over all growth and training, both athletic and intellectual, as he is the god of being sharpened by resistance. The
mythographer Herodorus even claims that Herakles was the
first philosopher: He obtained the "pillars of the earth" from
Atlas by learning natural law and obtained the apples of the
Hesperides which represent virtue. Fittingly, the proper way
of honoring Herakles is both simple and difficult: Commit
to disciplined self-betterment and to making sure that improvement sends positive ripples through your community
of friends and family. Each of the 12 labors was also an act of
service.

Great God Herakles, may you now come to hear our
prayers and give aid to your praisers.

Orphic Hymn 12 - Herakles

Stout-hearted Herakles, untamed and mighty,
Vast-handed Titan, invincible God
All deeds of valor are yours to delight in

You of many forms, kind, wise, and divine,
Gentle and endless, ineffable Father,
You Lord of All who sired Time

Many fall in earnest prayer
To you, the conquering archer and seer,
Omnivorous begetter, pinnacle and helper

For mankind's sake you tamed the tribes
Of savages who feared those arms
That uphold nurturing much-loved Peace

Unwearied blossom of most serene Earth,
Self-born and first-born in bright divine fire
You godly healer with gleaming scales

From East to West about your head
The sprawling dawn and dark night cling
To the circuit of labors, your twelve divine works

Reigning in Heaven, supremely skilled,
A boundless God amidst immortals,
With infinite, unshaken, blessed arms

May you come, holy one, attend to our prayer,
Wielding the mace to drive away evil,
And guard us from unrighteous fates

Herakles' Prayer

Son of Zeus, great and kind, with boundless arms,
Lord Herakles,
Surpassing all the many trials sent by mother Hera,
You came to know the God within,
That kernel of the absolute
Sprouted, and is loved by man forever

May you always turn our eyes towards the Gods,
Upwards and within, no matter what befalls the flesh,
And help us to attain a blessed Hebe of our own

Herakles' Prayer for Endurance

Herakles, Kallinikos, immortal son of Zeus
And friend to all mankind, for you yourself have felt
The trials of this earthly life,
May you ignite and staunchly tend
Unquenchable endurance
In my limbs and in my heart

Hephaistos

Vulcan, Hephaestus,

Hephaistos, the craftsman of the Gods, is the shaper of the forms that allow life to express itself structuredly. He is both the hammer and the fire of the forge, attesting to the nuclear structure of the cosmos as energy organized into atomic and sub-atomic structures. He is a supremely vivifying power who reminds us that the free and proper flow of force is not opposed to structure but is actually reliant on healthy and harmonious structures. Hephaistos is the son of Hera, as crafting a structure relies on the presence of divided parts whose differences provide shape and texture.

It was said mythologically that he was once thrown down from Olympus, either because of insubordination to Zeus in defense of Hera or because Hera was displeased at his club foot after conceiving him asexually. According to the first account, Hephaistos is born healthy but gets crippled when thrown down. Usually Hephaistos is considered the son of Zeus, but the latter myth exists for a few reasons. Firstly, it casts him as a counterpart to Athena. She is also concerned with the material world and its bodies, and Hephaistos is intertwined with her in several other myths, including her birth. Secondly, the myth of his fatherless birth is meant to show that the material world would be misshapen and unfit without the input and providence of Zeus.

When Hephaistos is thrown down to earth, representing the procession of divine form and fire from the highest to the lowest, he lands in the ocean's waters of life and is recovered by the sea-nymph Thetis. He is nursed back to health and raised by Thetis on the island of Lemnos, an echo of an episode of Hera's youth where she was raised by Tethys while in hiding from Kronos. On Lemnos Hephaistos takes up blacksmithing and quickly masters it, soon becoming famous for his weapons and jewelry. We should note the correspondence of Hephaistos plunging into the ocea to the act of a blacksmith quenching a newly-forged item in water and the symbolic similarity of the Sun descending below Oceanus at night. Hephaistos' arrival in the generative world is occasioned by the cooling of his fire and the settling of his substance, as was mentioned in discussion of Poseidon.

The gods on Olympus eventually hear of his smithing skill and ask him to return. He refuses, but sends a gift to Hera: a golden throne with invisible fetters. Hera sits in it and is trapped, but Hephaistos refuses to come and release her in anger for his abandonment. Here there are again two different accounts of the story.

According to one, Dionysos descends to earth to persuade him. Hephaistos trusts Dionysos because the latter has also quarrelled with Hera, and agrees to drink his wine. Dionysos then places the inebriated Hephaistos on a mule and brings him back to Olympus, where he frees his mother.

According to the other version, Zeus offers Aphrodite's hand in marriage to whoever frees Hera, not actually expecting Hephaistos to show his face after such a transgression. All the other gods try and fail to undo the fetters. Eventually Hephaistos hears of the prize and arrives at Olympus to free Hera himself, marrying Aphrodite to the other gods' chagrin.

These two versions of the myth offer different explanations for the cause of the same process, the reconciliation of the generated with its numinous source. The first account posits that Dionysos enables ascent by dissolving our instinctual apprehension about divine matters - think of people getting mired in the "problem of evil" or being uncomfortable with how divine law and their personal moralities may not align perfectly. The second account posits that the proper way to reconcile the higher and the lower is through love and admiration of beauty, which reveals the harmony of the universe and re-assimilates our soul to that harmony.

Hephaistos is a god of creativity and labor. He is the god of fire in both its productive and destructive senses, since the endurance of any structure depends as much on keeping it free of rust and bloat as it does on making it sturdy. As the husband of Aphrodite, he desires beauty and so seeks to replicate it in all of his creations. He should therefore be thanked and invoked whenever we wish to do the same, to create beauty and to imbue our work with meaning and longevity. Honor him with dedication to a craft, though the definition of craft can really be stretched here; You may consider your body and health or your relationships as structures which deserve affectionate attention and improvement.

Great Hephaistos, may you now come to hear our prayers and be pleased by our praise.

Orphic Hymn 66 - Hephaistos

Hearty Hephaistos, inexhaustible fire,
Fiercely gleaming, bringing flame,
You God who holds the torch in mighty hands

Deathless artisan, holy one,
The perfect foundation of your cosmic portion
Is wrought by you, Vulcan, great divine craftsman

All-consuming, all-subduing, all-creating, highest God
Aither, sun and moon and stars are all
Your limbs made plain to mortal eyes

All cities, all dwellings, all peoples and beasts
Belong to you, God who dwells in the living
And blesses us, mighty one, with your creation

Come, happy God, to receive our libations
That you may come gently to make our work joyful
And stay the savage rage of fire

For nature itself burns hot in our bodies;
May you make them strong and pleasing to Zeus
As you deftly work the forms with skillful mind

Hymn to Cosmic Hephaistos

The billowing smoke is the dance of the God
Gripping the hammer with hands of white fire
Burning, creating, reshaping, the passion
Of calloused skin on mighty palms
Belongs to Hephaistos who forges the spheres

In atoms and loins the Son of the Empress
Thunders forever with unbounded heat,
Subsisting in All as aithereal plasma,
The white-hot blood of souls and stars

Sleeping in mountains, awakened in bedsheets,
The spouse of Venus strikes with joy;
Each and every molten spark
Springs into a sacred Life

Hephaistos' Prayer

Unquenchable fire, source and creator,
Father Hephaistos, most cunning and skilled,
You who burns and shapes and fills,
We thank you for your godly works

May you, Hephaistos, hear our prayer
And help us to create and live
With a craftsman's skilled precision
And with bursting, driving force

Pan

Faunus

Pan is a curious figure. His name is thought to be derived from the Arcadian word for "shepherd," and he remains an important deity to pastoral life. He was soon associated with a second meaning of "pan," "all," and so was thought to patronize all of nature both domestic and wild. He was associated with pastoral Apollo because of the former etymology, but later philosophical and alchemical works would focus on the latter meaning.

Pan is often depicted wearing a ram's horns and with the hind legs of a goat. There is the obvious connection to sheep and goat herding, but symbols are rarely so one-dimentional. Horns are a common accoutrement meant to demonstrate instinctive natural power, appearing with the Helleno-Egyptian syncretism of Zeus-Ammon and in depictions of his son Alexander, who Muslims still refer to as "the Horned One." There is even a famous depiction of Moses wearing small horns on his head.

Pan's goat legs symbolize wildness and fertility. Later commenters would add that they are meant to communicate that the lower half of the cosmos, which Pan represents panentheistically, lacks Reason but abounds in growth and instinct. Of course the reason for this is that Becoming is an incomplete derivative of Being, though it can still be fun and somber denialism rarely does much good.

Another curious thing about Pan is the strange Romantic period renaissance of his worship, making him one of the earliest faces of neo-paganism, long before more historically-minded reconstructionist efforts became widespread. Artists and poets of the early 19th century found his naturalism, pantheism, and (seemingly to them) non-legalistic moral orientation to be strong contrasts to the dominant religions of the time. They weren't necessarily wrong, and Pan certainly seems suited to a life-affirming and informal method of worship. One can approach the God for anything regarding plant and animal life, the outdoors, celebration, and fertility. Honor him by making a point to include all of these things in your life and by offering gratitude for them.

Great God Pan, may you now come to hear our prayers and be joyed by them.

Orphic Hymn 11 - Pan

I call upon pastoral Pan, I call upon the cosmos,
I call upon the sky and sea and Earth the queen of all,
I call upon immortal fire, too, where Pan is Lord

Come, companion of the seasons, restless, blessed one,
Hooved and horned and revelling when weaving playful song
To set the world in harmony or rouse our dreadful fantasies

You delight in gushing fountains
And in springs where herdsmen gather,
You dance with nymphs and naiads,
Blessed hunter, Echo's lover

Dwelling in growth and in all things' begetting,
All-fertile ruler, cave-loving reveler,
Truly Zeus who bears stout horns,

The endless plain of Earth is held
Between your palms as the unwearied sea
Yields its deep-flowing waters around you

Earth-girding eddying Ocean surrenders
To hear your command, as does Air's swirling embers,
The breath of fire that kindles life

And high above the heavy earth
The most sublime Eye of aitherial flame
Bears witness to you as the most holy sovereign,
You who holds these planes apart

All things' natures submit to your providence,
Your bountiful Earth brings to mankind his nourishment,
And so may you come to receive the libation
And safeguard us a peaceful end

Pan's Prayer

Great lord Pan, giver of life and master of nature,
May you help me to witness you wherever you dwell
And to welcome your gifts and powers.
May you fill me with the joys of life,
Of growth and wild union,
And welcome me to join your revel-rout through hilly glens

Apollon

Phoebus Apollo, the Far-Darter

Apollo is an immensely important and wide-ruling god. His extremely varied activities can perhaps be described with a few abstract through-lines: Distance, balance, and vision. His associations range from wolves, hunting, and shepherding to prophecy, medicine, and philosophy. Throughout all of these activities he remains the far-shooting archer, the purifier, and the all-seeing one.

His worship seems to have undergone a great amount of elaboration over the centuries that eventually resulted in an image of a very civilized and even urban Apollo, but it should not be forgotten that he is the twin brother of Artemis and was considered a god of pastoralism early on. Such a position makes sense in relation to his associations with healing (caring for injured animals) and vision (spotting and warding off predators). It even fits with his association with music, which he shares with Pan and Hermes. Hermes especially is important to Apollo, aiding him in his role of bridging Zeus with his sublunar creation.

Apollo is the god of light. All light, not exclusively that of the sun. Light is not only the cause of vision but of life itself - according to the ancients, the distinction is extremely minor. Apollo's light illumines the sensible world just as Zeus illumines the numinous world. Thus Apollo is lord of prophecy; just as he makes divine aither into visible light, he makes the motions of the higher worlds understandable to those below.

In Philosophical terms Apollo can be seen as the intellective power in itself, held remote from its objects, seeing, judging, and forming "from afar," thus his silver bow. He is the predecessor of Soul, or at least the point at which Soul, ruled by Hermes, proceeds far enough into the divisible world to experience itself independently from the Intellect that sustains it. This distance accounts for why his myths frequently involve lost love; he is too transcendent to "grasp" or be bound to the things he witnesses, no matter how beautiful they are.

Apollo is always depicted as a beardless youth because he stands directly above the point at which space-time begins. This doesn't have to be a one-way trip; that's part of why Apollo is so important to us, as he accords both the ascent and the descent of the soul according to its virtue.

He is the god of both music and medicine for a single reason: he is the great harmonizer, a role he shares with Aphrodite and Hermes. Medicine is the art of harmonizing the body with itself, its environment, and its source, to which end Apollo sends his son Asclepius. The maintenance of that harmony, preventative care and healthy habits, then fall under the purvue of Asclepius' daughter Hygeia.

Music having cosmological significance has already been touched on in relation to Ymir, Odin, and the runes. The structure of music can teach us much about metaphysics; pitch corresponds to space and tempo to time. A song occurs in-between its lowest note and its highest, forming various different "shapes" as it travels along its course.

Harmony is considered holy because *harmony is the way unity expresses itself in a divided realm.* Thus Apollo, who translates divine light into sensible light, imposes harmony upon the lower world. This is his slaying of Python, which then enables him to speak his oracles.

Similarly Apollo enables the existence of Time, which we measure by the motions of the Sun, and Space, which we perceive because of the presence of light within it. This is because these two things are actually no less than the particular way in which infinity and eternity expresses themselves when they proceed into generation and into matter.

Apollo is the voice of Zeus and the leader of the Muses, goddesses of the arts and sciences who are daughters of the titaness Mnemosyne, Memory. The arts rely on Apollo as the great beholder and bringer of divine beauty, which it is the job of art to emulate. Mnemosyne is dear to Apollo because memory is the human faculty that most resists the shifting sands of time, attempting to imitate the atemporal omniscience of a god.

This connection grows more involved in light of Plato's idea of memory and recollection, which is that all learning is simply the remembrance of information that our soul, by means of its communion with the united cosmos, has inherent access to.

Apollo should be addressed for matters of art, purification, inspiration, divination, and healing. Honor him by taking up an instrument or an artistic hobby and by aiming to be moderate. Moderation doesn't really mean steely stoicism; it requires passion as well as the ability to control and marshal that passion. Apollo is Dionysos' big brother, not his opponent.

Lord Apollo, may you now come to hear our prayers and to illumine our lives.

Orphic Hymn 34 - Apollon

Come, blessed healer, you slayer of Tityos,
Phoebus Lykoreus, shining on Parnassus,
Memphian, famous, bliss-giving, lyre-bearing,
Titanic and pythian, fruitful generator,
And sminthian slayer of Python

Delphian prophet, wild and radiant,
Handsomest son and most glorious youth,
Far-darting Father, Master of Muses,
Cultivating blessed joys

Far-ruling prophet, holy Didymaeus,
You, lord of Delos, are the all-seeing eye,
The beholder through whom every mortal knows Light;
Golden-haired and speaking truths,
May you look well on our prayers for mankind

Through blessed earth and boundless Aither
And even star-flecked shifting Night
You gaze upon the stout foundation
Roots below, the bounds of All

The first and the last, the start and the finish,
Lie in your palm as the limbs of a bow;
And with those strings, your blessed lyre,
You cause all things to bloom

Yours is the axis of Heaven, resounding
With sounds of the lyre as it sings your commands,
Drawing all things into their righteous balance

For here you play the lowest pitch,
And there you play the highest,
And here you play a doric tune
To set the poles in harmony
And preserve diverse tribes of mankind and beasts

In every mortal heart you infuse
A fair, balanced share of both summer and winter,
Three strings for one and three more for the other,
And a lovely blooming spring when you come
To hear our voices, happy God

For all men call you, Jovian lord,
Rutting Pan who sends the winds
And forms the whole of the weighty Cosmos

Hymn to Apollon Pythoktonos

Astride those swirling depths did you of unshorn hair
Drive that vicious bolt to shatter Python's head
That fatal head
Which teemed with gushing venom
Venom pooling high in valleys
And coursing in rivers to stain the white ankles of naiads

Atop the spiral coil of his victim did beloved Phoebus stamp
That cleated sandal, silent with serene triumph;
Then the darting Lord with sheer command
Opened wide the mouth of Earth,
Shut tight to earnest prophecy

You lowered down the vanquished one to rot amidst
The jagged teeth of stone and fleshy dirt which furnish now
That tongue of Earth, the serpent drake, that fruitful branch
Who ripens Heaven's counsel
Just as muscle blooms from seed

Hymn to Phanaeus Apollon

You, the Sun and all the stars
As King is Crown and Throne,
As center-seed contains whole fruit
And all its life, one timeless point

A center has no matter - this, your gravity,
Fountain spouting light and vigor,
Filling every lived-in Thing

Light Your fire over Delphi,
Sprint Your ranging Caucasus,
Speak Your verse; let healing runes
Ring clear in open council-rooms

Axis turning wider circles,
Python slain upon his wheel,
Touch circumference with your youthful
Force; Such stillness overflows

Fountain spouting light and vigor
Knowing, seeing all the Forms,
Intellect, and Point, and Line,
Apollon, God who tramples time

Hymn to Delphic Apollon

And then the darting Lord dispensed
From Zeus his holy father's throne
These words for sons of men to hear,
These words for pious men to heed:

"Where are your songs, and where are your priests?
What do you give, and what will you keep?
What are the rites for which the sun rises,
And do your prayers like orchards sprout
Up from fertile, praiseful mouth?"

Tight-strung bow and lyre, my God,
Are yours to wield; so let resound
The arrow which is python's fall,
The music which is heaven's call:

"Here will all the rightly-led with skillful hands
Be given the songs which I gave once to Man,
Here will I teach that greatest of joys,
The joy of the well-practiced offering-rite,
Just as Sun himself hastens to offer His light"

Apollo's Prayer

Lord Apollo, Artist, Archer, striking from afar,
Revealing and resounding, working chords of harmony,
Relentlessly you draw all things away from void,
Protecting and inspiring those who look towards the Gods

And so may you inspire now, and always gently guide
Our hands and minds in art and song
So that our works will all align with Zeus' tireless law

Apollo's Prayer for Purification

Lord Apollo, Smintheus,
Darting sunlit king,
May you who strikes down evil
With your arcing tight-strung bow
Descend to cleanse our altars, homes, and souls

Apollo's Prayer for Health

Lord Apollo, healthful youth, athletic and untiring,
Shining source of harmony, Jovian fountain of life,
May you look kindly on my prayer
And grant me overflowing health, hardy and harmonious,
And beauty of all kinds most pleasing,
Within me and without

Balder

The Bright One

Balder is a god of light, purity, and unity. He is described as having a calm, gentle, and honorable character. Because of this the gods loved and respected him more than any other, an affection that was especially strong in his mother Frigge.

The one preserved myth about him, the famous tale of his killing, is largely a naturalistic allegory for the cycle of the year; the brutish winter-god Hodr accidentally slays Balder, his twin brother, using the evergreen (and parasitic) mistletoe. Balder descends to Helheim, where he remains until he is released at Ragnarok, the end of the greater cycle.

Balder gives us an appropriate occasion to discuss Ragnarok, as it's a significant doctrinal departure from the mediterranean traditions. It seems to align with teachings from certain hindu schools that as the manifest cosmos progresses through the yugas and is eventually annihilated and reborn, certain "lower" devas undergo the same process and reemerge in the next cycle as different beings but molded in the same "pattern" as those from the last cycle.

Really what separates this doctrine from those of Greece and Rome is an essential difference in ideas regarding what a god is and does, as the Hellenistic system posits that every major God effects but is unaffected, moves but is unmoved, creates but is uncreated. Even if the entire cosmos were to un-manifest, which is possible, then its re-emergence would be structurally identical even if certain events unfolded differently because the Gods contain the laws of nature and the principles of creation eternally within them like the genes inside a seed.

It is possible that the ancient Germans understood the cultic and mythic structures of their gods to be totems that themselves undergo generation and decay but which represent intelligences that are free from those things. Thus "Tyr" may "die" but "that which causes and performs what we have labeled Tyr" does not. We also unfortunately have no good way of knowing just how extensive christian meddling in the transmission of these narratives was, and we can hardly expect the christ cult to record its competitors fairly, at least not until comparative religion comes on the scene in the modern centuries.

In any case, what is important regarding Balder is that he is a unifying force. At the behest of Frigge, all things in existence except for the mistetoe, which was too young, swore an oath to never harm Balder. Thus the killing of Balder is the first act of Ragnarok because it is the loss of light and unity in this world. The crisis is almost averted when Hel declares that she will release him if all things in existence weep for him, restoring unity. Everything, especially the remorseful mistletoe, weeps - except for Loki.

Balder is the father of Forseti, the god of justice and of right counsel at assemblies, which requires the unified concord of the people present. As the son of Odin and Frigge, the creator and the proliferator, Balder could be called "God of unifying the separated" moreso than a being whose unifying power is prior to multiplicity. Balder's death causes Odin to create Vali, who matures in less than a day and kills Hodr in revenge. This may be to show that when cosmic law is knocked off-balance it corrects itself forcefully, in a way that often seems vengeful.

Balder is also linked to at least three runes. The first is the fire-rune Kauna, ‹. Kauna is the rebirth of the sacrifice in fire, of its transfer from a physical object to an energetic pattern offered in devotion. In this way it is an illuminating and enlightening fire. It is also the rune of crafting, of the combination of two things to produce an aesthetically and functionally coherent and appealing third.

The second is Wunjo, ᛈ, which evokes the unifying power of joy & the power of unity to evoke joy. It is also the rune of continuity & connection between things which share a source. Balder, the son of the high God and Goddess, can be said to share his origin with all of creation and is therefore positioned to be the power of joyful unity between all things.

The third rune is Dagaz, ᛞ, the rune of daytime, and specifically of the balance between night and day. Balder's journey through both realms guarantees this balance, a balance that unifies all that is involved and which produces the spark of inspiration and understanding for which Balder's light is loved.

Balder should be addressed for protection, purification, and social concord. Honor him by being gentle and patient as well as courageous and even-minded in the face of fate. Seek to create, maintain, and reconcile good relationships.

Great Balder, may you now come to hear our prayers, and may you bring us joy and awe.

Baldersong

A torch burns hot in blackness,
Ulcer in exile from Balder;
Defiant flame may earn great fame
So far from its father

A God descends in mistletoe,
A God comes forth in fire,
A God brings light from Helheim's depths
To quell the weeping choir

Bliss is clear view's open field
And bright skies unencumbered;
Prospers he who draws Him near
That shines as bright as thunder

A God descends in mistletoe,
A God comes forth in fire,
A God brings light from Helheim's depths
To quell the weeping choir

The day is joy to shield-kin,
The night is joy to lovers,
Balder is the joy of all
Who call great Frigge "Mother"

A God descends in mistletoe,
A God comes forth in fire,
A God brings light from Helheim's depths
To quell the weeping choir

Balder's Prayer for Purification

Balder, great forgiving God, Brightly shining prince,
May you with most exceeding light come gently to my prayer
To cast away all darkness and all things that mean us harm,
For all upon the earth have vowed
To never breach your shield,
And we are greatly thankful when we fall beneath its guard

Helios

Sol

Helios, the illuminator, is especially concerned with vision and with consistency, which he treasures as the keeper of oaths. Helios is the driver of the orb of the Sun, guaranteeing its orderly and unflinching progression through the cosmos and through the wheel of the year. Helios guarantees the incarnate Self as a pattern of action and habits as well as the esoteric, unmanifest Self as the thing which beholds its own effects below.

Originally considered a benevolent Titan, his worship would eventually become involved in several different syncretisms. Really, many if not most Gods could be considered "Solar" thanks to their luminary nature, and we may now recall the brief discussion in the introduction of Henads and the possibility of gods subsisting in each other reflectively.

The most common syncretisms of Helios were with Apollo and with Zeus/Jupiter. Both of these were in vogue in the Roman Imperial period moreso than in classical Greece, and Zeus-Helios as Sol Invictus was especially popular in the waning days of the empire. Zeus-Helios was the favorite god of Emperor Julian the Blessed, as well as being important to the late Platonist schools. The Neoplatonists held that the orb of the sun served as the ideal physical representation of the form of the Good, making all lower things intelligible to us by way of our own souls' fundamental sympathy with it.

Helios is never far from us. He should be propitiated in matters of honor and fair conduct as well as foresight and vision, as he reveals the connectedness of things in the karmic web which he transcends and illumines. Honor him with honesty, responsibility, willpower, and curiosity.

Fleet lord Helios, may you now descend to receive our thanks and prayers, and may you illumine for us the most righteous paths.

Mesomedes of Krete's
Hymn to the Sun

You are the father of the snowflake
Riding the rosy chariot
Pulled by fleet horses,
With golden hair and happy
To cross the bounds of Ouranos

Your spinning rays the sources
Of all light and love of wisdom,
Traversing Gaia's face entire,
Rivers of undying fire
Give birth to lovely Day

Around you stars are dancing
for the King of wide Olympus,
Forever singing joyous songs
To match the lyre of Phoebus

And gray Selene beneath you
Measures out the course of months
Drawn by shining silver bulls
While your gentle mind is satisfied
To look upon the cosmos

Helios' Prayer

Father Sun, Beholder, blessed eye and blessed giver,
May you illumine all good things,
Beget them in your likeness,
And with gentle fire rinse away
Disease, dishonor, and illusion

Mithras

Mitra, Mithra

Mithras is a curiously ancient and foreign God who's narrowly made it into this book thanks to the interesting late imperial heyday of the Roman Mithraic Mysteries. Mithras entered Roman religious life via the Persian east, but the oldest records of him are actually Vedic. In the Roman cult he's the guide of individuals towards unity with him and is also connected to Sol Invictus in a cooperative manner. For the Vedics he was slightly more aloof, being the partner of Varuna who guaranteed Rta, the natural order. These are both gods of light, and it was said that Mitra illumined the dawn and Varuna dusk. The procession of the day is one of the most immanent examples of Rta in our lives, so their involvement is fitting.

Mitra would also come to be associated with friendship, a facet that perhaps influenced his adoption by Roman military men who organized tight-knit communities around his worship. Although Mitra, now called Mithras after some translation through Persia, was the centerpiece of these cult lodges, the actual content of the rites seems to have been pretty solidly occidental or at least Mediterranean. In them Mithras seems to take on either a demiurgic or salvific role with his killing of a bull (Tauroctony), which is the climax and focal point of his mythology.

Mithras, after being born from a stone, which he then strikes to bring forth water, goes through great pains to subdue a cosmic bull. This bull may have thematic connections to Audhumla and to the conjectured Proto-Indo-European story of Manu and Yama establishing mankind with the sacrifice of a cow. The scene of the Tauroctony is littered with astrological references, often having the Sun, Moon, and five planets situated above Mithras. There is also usually a dog, crow, and scorpion present, as well as ears of grain growing out of the bull. The grain may suggest that Mithras creates the earth out of the bull or that he fertilizes the earth with it.

Following the sacrifice Mithras ascends to the heavens to meet with Helios, suggesting that the Mithraic mysteries essentially offer a method of reenacting Mithras' deeds so that the initiate may ascend. Whether the goal was immortality, enlightenment, or simple fulfillment is unfortunately unclear as much as been lost to time or was kept secret.

Mithras should be called on for matters of comradery, oathkeeping, and success in the personal spiritual journey of subduing whatever might cause us to act dishonorably. Honor him with optimism, friendship, enthusiasm, and the establishment of order in your own life.

Great Mithras, may you now come to hear our prayers and guide our hands.

Rig Veda Hymn 59 - Mitra
translated by Ralph Griffith

Mitra, when speaking, stirreth men to labour:
Mitra sustaineth both the earth and heaven.

Mitra beholdeth men with eyes unclosing.
To Mitra bring, with holy oil, oblation.

Foremost be he who brings thee food, O Mitra,
Who strives to keep thy sacred Law, Āditya.

He whom thou helpest ne'er is slain or conquered,
On him, from near or far, falls no affliction.

Joying in sacred food and free from sickness,
With knees bent lowly on the earth's broad surface,

Following closely the Āditya's statute,
May we remain in Mitra's gracious favour.

Auspicious and adorable, this Mitra was born
With fair dominion, King, Disposer.

May we enjoy the grace of him the Holy, yea,
Rest in his propitious loving-kindness.

The great Āditya, to be served with worship,
Who stirreth men, is gracious to the singer.

To Mitra, him most highly to be lauded,
Offer in fire oblation that he loveth.

The gainful grace of Mitra, God,
Supporter of the race of man,
Gives splendour of most glorious fame.

Mitra whose glory spreads afar,
He who in might surpasses heaven,
Surpasses earth in his renown.

All the Five Races have repaired to Mitra, ever strong to aid,
For he sustaineth all the Gods.

Mitra to Gods, to living men,
To him who strews the holy grass,
Gives food fulfilling sacred Law.

Hymn to Mithras

Who! Who among you can tell me the name
Of that intimate glow in the halls of savage kings?
It ripens like long, soft grass
Swaying in praise under Mithras' daring smile;

His is the joy of a warband's friendship,
Love made Oath in taurine gore,
And His is the eye that beholds vast Aion
Aither made fruitful in Time's fleet swirl

Mithra's Purification Prayer
Donated to this project by Mithridates

O Mithra, cleanser of Miasma,
Wash away the filth and sin from your loyal follower
So that I may be heard rightly

Artemis

Diana, the Huntress

The maiden huntress, the liminal mistress of spirits, the Left Eye of Zeus, Artemis is a goddess with very a broad set of activities. The briefest distillation of their common goal is to say that Artemis animates-through-boundaries, establishing limits between forms and creatures so that they have their own domains and lives through which to express themselves.

Alongside Hera and Demeter, Artemis is part of the triad responsible for animating the cosmos by translating being, life, and intellect into the multiplicity that we experience. Hera, translating Zeus' Being, is often depicted as distant and constant. Demeter, translating the fire of raw, basic life, is concerned with everything from microbes to crops to full humans. Finally Artemis, translating her brother Apollo's intellect, is specifically concerned with the life cycle of sentient creatures like animals and humans, imparting individual intellects upon them. She governs both their births as a midwife & their deaths as a huntress, as death clears the way for new birth.

Artemis holds within herself the wellspring of the highest forms of earthly life and intelligence, and so she is also important as a healing Goddess. Where Apollo heals by harmony, restoring balance, Artemis heals by driving the constructive powers inherent in souls to grow and re-grow. For this reason, as well as her role in childbirth, she is considered the special patroness of children and youths.

Artemis is an important fertility deity, which may seen counterintuitive with her near-universal depiction as a virgin. Her virginity is symbolic of of youth, self-ownership, and as a segue to our next point, boundaries.

Artemis is a liminal Goddess, holding within herself the boundary between forest & field, life & death, sex & continence. Accordingly, many of her rites were actually erotic or libidinal, meant to approach boundaries without breaking them. This association with boundaries also positions her as a stringent enforcer of natural and karmic law, which is part of the reasoning for her depiction as a huntress; predation is the law of the jungle and is exremely important to ecological health.

It's hard to overstate how intimately intertwined Artemis is with her brother Apollo. They are a divine pair on par in importance with Freyr and Freya, and nearly even matching Zeus and Hera. Indeed they echo that same pair. The Sun and the Moon, the two astrological "luminaries," are the eyes of Zeus as described in the Orphic Rhapsody. Through them the numinous world illumines ours and in so doing experiences it with us. This is part of Artemis' activity of animation. She is just as much a deity of light as Apollo is. For this reason Artemis and goddesses near to her are often depicted with torches and with epithets like "Phosphora." As mentioned earlier, since Artemis animates-through-boundaries she is seen as a more nocturnal light, a light within darkness that offers a passageway back to the all-pervading light of Apollo's day.

Artemis should be addressed in matters of hunting, childbirth and childcare, and personal health and motivation. Literal hunting may not be accessible for many of us anymore, but there are lots of activities that share its essence; Exercise, especially running, sprinting, and high-impact workouts, chasing goals, career or otherwise, and even chasing mates. Above all, though, honor her by learning to spot the little moments where her activities shine through. Moments of birth, focus, victory, wildness, connectedness with nature, contact with the uncanny, these are all moments when Artemis draws near to share her gifts. Learn to welcome her when she comes.

Great maiden Artemis, may you now incline to our prayers, and may you be greatly pleased by them.

Orphic Hymn 36 - Artemis

Hear me, O Goddess, Olympian Daughter,
Bacchic, titanic, exalted darting huntress,
Torch-bearing Phosphora, midwife and maiden,
Protectress of children and ripening women,
Painless goddess, easing pains, zeal-igniting, driving away
All cares like pests who haunt the fields

Youthful sprinter, archer, huntress,
Roaming through the glossy night,
Keeper of chapels, gracious liberator,
Wailing in revels, bestowing births,
You who fosters fledgling mortals

Fond of the chase, immortal yet earthly, slaying beasts,
Blessed waxer of wild fruits,
Dwelling in forests and high on proud mountains,
You heiress of all, beautiful queen,
Eternally sprinting with dogs through the trees

Many-shaped goddess, Soteira, please come
With open ear and gentlest heart to our song
And deliver to your faithful praisers
The fruits of the earth, lush hair and good health,
And peace, may you drive all our woes to the hills
Where you rush to destroy them, rejoicer-in-kills

Hymn to Soul-Bearing Artemis

Filling chests with white hot breath to pour into the living,
Animatrix, Midwife, Maiden, filling Zeus' vast creation,
I call to you with grateful heart

Filling limbs with coursing acid burning hot like wine,
Sprinter, Darter, Hunter, Killer,
Cutting weak flesh off the vine,
I call to you who dwells in strength

Filling eyes with trembling fire
Leaping through the midnight air,
Your silver torches glisten in the stomach of the bear,
I call to you whose crown brings light

Filling heads with stark fixation, spiral-chasing Intellect,
Knower, Seer, Prophetess, O sister of the Delphic Prince,
I call to You who fills the world, I call to holy Artemis

Artemis' Prayer for Health

Lady Artemis, darting maiden,
Striking daughter of highest Zeus,
Torch-bearer, life-giver, midwife and huntress,
Protectress of children, ecstatic shining warden,
May you hear my prayer to you
And fill my heart, my eyes and skin,
And all my limbs and flowing hair
With glowing health to mirror your own

Idun

Iðunn, Iduna

Idun, the keeper of the golden apples of immortality, is the goddess of youth and is somewhat cognate with Hebe. She also has possible connections to Greek Eos and Anglo-Saxon Eostre. Idun herself is characterized as gentle, carefree, and youthful, but the majority of her relevant symbology is tied up with the golden apples that she presides over, apples which the Gods mythologically rely on for their immortality.

The apple, in general, is a symbol of youth, health, and love. All fruits attest to a central mystery of life: The procession from seed to tree to fruit to seed. It is revealed that the seed produces itself, but in doing so first manifests as the tree, the bony structure of reality, and then as the fruit, the watery food which feeds the seed as it again becomes a tree.

That seed is the seed that the Vedantic sage Uddalaka ordered his son Svetaketu to split smaller and smaller until it could be split no more, before he then uttered the famous words "Tat tvam asi," "That, thou art." Idun's apples are none other than the flesh that feeds the Absolute as it proceeds from itself back into itself, sustaining the series and symbols suspended from the Gods as it does so.

The primary myth involving Idun is her kidnapping by Thiazi, who coerces Loki into luring her over Bifrost out of Asgard. The Aesir then order Loki to recover Idun, which he does by transforming into a falcon and sneaking into Thiazi's lair. When he finds her, he transforms her into an acorn and flees the lair. Thiazi gives chase in the form of an eagle, and Loki defeats him by luring him into a wall of fire the Aesir had set up. This myth essentially highlights the importance of Idun to the Gods and thus the world, but it also reenacts the life cycle of a seed; origin, departure, and return. It outlines the importance of the human mind to this cycle as represented by Loki, who is responsible both for the fall and the rescue.

Idun can be connected to two runes: Gebo, X, "Gift", and Perthro, ᛈ, "Pear-tree" or "Dice-cup". Gebo, straightforwardly, is the pathway of reciprocity between higher and lower, between first seed and second. Along this pathway grow the roots and branches of the world-tree, branches that carry the force that becomes the fleshy fruit around future seeds.

Perthro is more enigmatic. It represents a vessel through which the absolute projects itself into the soluble world by way of fate, law, and time. As such, its mystery is central to its meaning. It is the rune of curiosity, from which we cast the lots of divination, and we may even compare it symbolically to the biblical Eve's fruit of knowledge. Perthro is Idun's basket, in which she carries the fruit of the runes, the powers that feed the absolute's worldly manifestation.

It is good to approach Idun for matters of health, general happiness, adaptation to the flow of the seasons, and recognition of the unchangeable absolute within oneself. Honor her by cultivating joy, youthfulness, and generosity in your own life.

Divine Idun, may you now come to hear our prayers and to take joy in our gift of praiseful words.

Hymn to Idun

Giver of the golden fruit
That blooms in evening's jaws,
Giver of the youthful fruit
That seizes each new dawn

Giver of the flesh that falls
From heavy branch at dusk,
Giver of the seed that sprouts
To greet the rising sun

Bearer of the serpent-skin
That sheds and is discarded,
Bearer of the dragon-eyes
That witness all and guard it

Giver of the youth of babes,
Preserver of the Gods,
Giver of the blissful sleep
Beneath ancestral mounds

Where Woden stirs between the eyes
To watch Himself uncoil
And witness Youth emerging
Ever-new from loosened soil

Idun, Goddess, blessed mother,
Sister, daughter, friend,
May you with gleaming hands destroy
The writhing veil of the End

Idun's Prayer

Great Iduna, apple-bearing, bringing joyful youth to all,
We thank you for your gentle gifts
And for the truths you glibly teach;
May you draw us near
So that our hearts stay young and fruitful.

Selene

Luna, Phoebe, The Moon

Selene is, straightforwardly, the Moon. She is linked to Artemis in the same way that the Sun is linked to Apollo. The moon is the final luminary body, the one nearest to the earth, and the one which appears to move fastest through the sky. Consequently it is generally the body whose movements' effects are most acutely felt on earth.

The ancients believed the moon to be the "bottom of heaven", the point at which the perfect, unchanging, numinous power of heaven descended into the temporal world. Thus our world was called "sublunar", because we are under the realm and sway of the moon. Of course in modernity we can understand this is not literal, but it is symbolically very resonant in the ways that matter.

Selene rules many things; The passage of time and seasons, cycles of rebirth, and the aquatic subconscious and "lower" soul to name a few. She is both a force of animation and a boundary between modes of being, appropriate to her connection with Artemis. Unlike Artemis she is not considered a virgin in the mythology, and there are many tales of Selene taking on different lovers and rearing children.

Like Helios, Selene has been extensively syncretized and swapped into or out of many different myths involving a goddess figure. She is, of course, a strongly astrological goddess whose worship is infuenced by the apparent phases of the moon. She may be addressed for guidance and protection, especially in internal or emotional matters.

Divine Selene, may you now come to hear our prayers and look well on our praises.

Orphic Hymn 9 - Selene

Hear me, O Selene, light-bringing and divine,
You bull-horned Moon, crossing through the air
Swiftly by night locked in race with the darkness

Nocturnal and torch-bearing, great starlit maiden,
Waxing and waning, Androgynous Moon
And most luminous lover of horses

Mother of time and bearer of fruits,
Moody with an amber hue
And shining bright amidst the stars

All-seeing, vigilant, delighting in quiet,
And revelling in nighttime's richness
Granting your favor with jewel-like brightness

Long-coated leader of Night's shining bodies
Highest wise maiden with cyclical dance,
Come, Great Selene, blessed and gentle

Lady of stars, with your own luminosity,
Shine upon your new devotees,
And with your brightness, maiden, save them

Selene's Prayer

Great Selene, warden of the realm of night,
May you illumine all within
So that no wicked thought or deed will come to pass
Unexamined and unimpeded

Skadi

Mistress of Borderlands

It was said of Skadi that she was a giantess who joined the Aesir by marrying Njorth. In fact she was said to be the daughter of Thiazi, the etin who kidnapped Idun. She had traveled to Asgard for revenge, but instead Odin offered her the chance to marry any of the gods. The caveat was that the gods would be hidden except for their feet and shins when she chose. She hoped to pick Balder, but instead chose the feet of Njorth. This episode is perhaps meant to symbolize that an embodied soul has difficulty telling the difference between divinity expressing itself immanently versus transcendentally.

Skadi straddles the border between Asgard and Utgard just as the Moon designates the point of immersion for divine force entering our world. Unlike the Moon, Skadi is more concerned with preserving the barrier than passing through it, which makes her a purifying force who complements the work of generative deities like Njorth or Idun. Skadi is associated with winter, and her worship seems to be in large part apotropaic; Like Thor, Skadi's proximity to the etins makes her an effective foe to them.

Skadi's powers may be tied to at least three runes: Hagalaz, ᚺ, Naudiz, ᚾ, and Isa, ᛁ. All three of these runes share themes of constructive restriction and the harshness of reality.

Hagalaz, "hail," is the rune of a rising soul confronting both its own old patterns and lifeways and the sometimes harsh demands that future growth makes of it. As icy hail melts into fresh water, Hagalaz reveals the helpful nestled within the harmful just as the etin Skadi makes herself useful to the divine order.

Naudiz, "Need," is the rune of resistance that elicits strength via opposition. This rune maintains the tension of equal and opposite reactions that allows all things to exist, and reminds us that everything that exists is a necessary result of the laws and structures of the cosmos. Skadi, enforcing the distinction between the changing and the unchanging, is an excellent example of fruitfulness following from restriction, since her icy boundary keeps the manifest world from being flooded and dissolved by an excess of fire.

Isa, Ice, is the rune of stillness, focus, and identity. It is this force that interacts with Muspellheim's fires to calm and slow them down to the point that they produce first the forms and then the material world. Isa is present in the transformative cycle of Hagalaz and is one of the main "antagonists" against which Naudiz compels beings to press in order to sharpen them. Isa draws us closer to our self-construct, which can be helpful in some circumstances but dangerous in others. I would argue that in the age of excessive, disjointed, and high-speed media, most people are in need of Isa.

Skadi should be addressed in matters of protection, discipline, and focus. These subjects can be applied to many endeavors; the worldly, the spiritual, the artistic, etc. In all of them Skadi's specific activities have some small share.

Great Skadi, may you now come to hear our prayers and receive our thanks.

Hymn to Skadi

Skadi is the mountain stream,
The Goddess is the tree,
Skadi strikes down savage beasts
And skis the slopes with ease

Hail is the purest grain,
The arrow reaches far,
Wheeled fate may travel straight
yet drift on ice and stick in tar

Skadi is the mountain peak,
The Goddess wields Law,
Odin's law, relentless,
Dripping from the serpent's maw

Let what is done be done tenfold,
And ice's slipping coat of rime
Be fatal bridge to treachery
And friend to those who guide the blind

Skadi's Prayer

Divine Skadi, purifier, protector,
May you grand me the wisdom to know my limits
And the strength to always challenge them

Hekate

Goddess of Roads, Spirits, and Wisdom

It will be risky to speak of Hekate because this is a Goddess with an insanely immense depth and breadth of both scholarly and devotional work pertaining to her. This is a body of information which I could hardly do justice, but I will note that a large portion of it concerns magic moreso than religion, even if these topics are related.

Hekate is, in many ways, a stranger. Ruling liminal space and transition, Hekate is to the underworld as Artemis is to the woods. While the danger of the woods is fruitful and relatively accessible to humans, the boundary between over- and under-world is more important to preserve, and so Hekate acts more remotely or peripherally. Indeed she is often described as working from afar, which suits the apparent origin of her cultus in Anatolian sun worship that connected her to Apollo and Helios.

Hekate is often depicted in threes. Three heads, three dogs, three worlds under her influence, three pathways when she is Trivia, etc. She is also closely tied to Artemis, Selene, and Persephone, to such a degree that some consider them to operate as one unit.

Within the Artemis-Selene-Hekate triad, Hekate could be seen as a preserving force. While Artemis births things and Selene ripens and matures them, Hekate keeps them free of improper influences, as she is the hormetic and homeopathic mistress of beasts and spirits. At the same time Hekate ensures the smooth continuation of the cyclical motions of the worlds, evoking Persephone's immortality-within-perishability.

Hekate is also concerned with learning and information, especially useful information. This is likely part of how she accrued such a strong association with magic and the natural sciences, as well as strong devotion from many later Neoplatonists. In fact, there is a fragmentary myth where Hekate and Hermes engage in a hunting competition, with Hekate earning a new epithet after she beats him.

Hekate's importance to the ancient world seems to reach its zenith with the Chaldean Oracles, a set of theological texts which were believed to be the channeled words of Hekate and Helios-Apollo, along with a few other gods making minor appearances. In the system put forth by these texts Hekate serves as the supreme Goddess, cognate to Rhea or Hera. She emanates from the "First Father," who approximates the Supreme Principle, and gives birth to the "Second Father" who produces the intelligible world.

In the scheme of the Oracles Hekate is at the center of all things, is the mediator of all things, exists fully within the Empyreal (noetic), Spiritual, and Physical worlds, and illuminates the way for souls to proceed back towards the Supreme

Principle. Thus in late antiquity she was worshipped as a savior, Soteira, in a more thorough sense than she had been before as a ward against ill health and hostile spirits.

Hekate may be approached for matters of wisdom, guidance, divination, protection, and contact with the foreign or uncanny. Honor her with learning, especially spiritual learning. You can start by learning more about her than I am able to transmit here. She will send you down many interesting rabbitholes, and I've already been distracted from writing for too long researching this one Goddess.

Mother Hekate, may you now come to hear our prayers and be pleased by them, and may you guide us always towards greater understanding.

Orphic Hymn 1 - Hekate

Hekate of the roads, Hekate,
She of triple crossroads I invoke.

In Heaven, Earth, and Ocean,
The saffron-veiled queen revels
In the souls of the entombed

Perses' daughter, haunting wastes,
Canine queen, nocturnal,
Taking joy in wild deer
And eating your share of beasts, uncouth

Mistress of bulls, all the world's queen,
Mountain nymph, you guide and roam,
And care for growing youths

Maiden, I beg you, come fast to these rites,
Bearing your most joyous heart
And favor forever the oxherd

Proclus' Hymn to Hekate and Zeus-Janus

Hail the many-named mother of Gods,
Blessed with fair offspring, great Prothyreia,
Hail Hekate, effulgent in strength
And hail to you, forefather Janus,
Hail, invincible, most supreme Zeus

May you cause the course of my life
To shine and be laden with blessed things,
And may you drive disease away,
Far from me and all my limbs;

Call to my soul as it wildly rages,
Once it has passed through your mind-rousing rites
And pull it near when it is pure

Outstretch your hands, I beg you, and show me,
Show my needful heart the paths
That it is righteous for Gods to reveal;
I will observe with careful attention
The light through which dark births' lament may be fled

Outstretch your hands, I beg you, and bring me
Upon your soft winds to Eusebia's bay,
For I am exhausted and call out in need

Hail the many-named mother of Gods,
Blessed with fair offspring, great Prothyreia,
Hail Hekate, effulgent in strength
And hail to you, forefather Janus,
Hail, invincible, most supreme Zeus

Hekate's Prayer for Protection

Mother Hekate, driver of daimones, shepherding souls,
May you preserve for me a path,
Divinely lit, through earthly troubles

Hekate's Prayer for Guidance

Great triple Goddess, Hekate Trivia,
May you guide my hands and mind
So that I may behold the good
And through it, know what must be known

Hermes

Mercury, the Messenger

Hermes, also known as Mercury, is the messenger of Zeus. He's a very complicated & important god, but the most profound way to describe him is also one of the simplest possible - He travels. Wherever there are two things, he's zipping back and forth between them. The nature of his travels can be religious, mercantile, playful, deceitful, erotic, competitive, and much more, all illustrated in his rich mythos.

The most illustrative myth of Hermes' nature and activities is the story of his birth as told in the Homeric hymns. Hermes was born to Maia, a daughter of Atlas, in Arcadia. Mere hours after his birth he wandered out of his cave and used a tortoise shell and sheep tendons to create the first lyre. He then wandered off and eventually came to Apollo's pasture where the God's cattle were grazing. Hermes stole fifty of Apollo's cattle and then cooked two of them. Apollo discovered Hermes' mischief and took the infant to Olympus to face trial before Zeus for his crime. Zeus convinced Hermes to confess and lead Apollo to his stolen cattle.

When the two gods arrived at the outcropping where Hermes hid the cattle, Apollo was upset to discover two of his cattle already cooked. Hermes covered his tracks by dividing the meat into twelve equal portions and declaring he had prepared it as an offering to the Gods, thus performing the first sacrificial rite. This placated Apollo, who was content to collect the remaining 48 cows.

As Apollo did so, Hermes grew bored and began to play on his lyre. Apollo was immediately intrigued and offered to trade his entire herd of cattle for the lyre, to which Hermes agreed. Zeus then made Hermes the messenger of the gods on the condition that Hermes promised to never again tell a lie, and thus he joined the Olympians.

Alongside Apollo and Aphrodite, Hermes is one of the three cosmic harmonizers; he pertains to connections, unifying things that have been divided. He rules the dynamicity of the bond and how the bond manifests itself in the nodes it connects. Hermes is the ping-ponging of cause and effect between two connected centers, and in this way he establishes language itself. The word encodes information so that it can travel; Hermes ferries the word from mind to mind via mouth, air, and ear, and once it arrives the receiving mind uses its own embedded system of cognitive connections to sort and incorporate the new info.

This brings me to a point which is acknowledged even in modern astrology, which is that Hermes as Mercury is responsible for thought itself, at least the thought performed by our sublunar incarnated bodies. Hermes, though, is also responsible for the thought done by *systems*, which may today make us think of AI. This systems-thinking actually includes civilization itself; What is a civilization if not an intelligence, debatably artificial, whose computing is distributed across the hardware of its constituent institutions and populations? The thinking of a civilization is carried out by the speech and dialogue of its constituents between each other. This is by no means an egalitarian process, though, and we see Hermes closely associated with games, competitions, and sports - ways of sorting merit hierarchies.

Speaking of dialogue, Hermes is also of course the founder of religion. More specifically, he establishes the communicative nature of worship, carrying our prayers up from the pyre to his father's ear. Hermes is the bridge between lower and higher. Religion as we recognize it, as a reflective symbolic and linguistic image-complex which corresponds to otherwise incommunicable realities, must be doubly Hermetic in the civilized, incarnate world, but even in a primal state such as referenced by Hesiod's golden age Hermes would still be responsible for communion and for whatever "transitions" could be said to happen in such a simple and unified state.

As the bridge between higher and lower, matter and Intellect, Hermes is the leader, the serial fountainhead, of Soul in the specifically Neoplatonic sense. This is because Soul is the intermediary between the unchanging Intellect and ever-changing matter and therefore becomes the first layer of godhead which could be said to be mobile, interacting with time and space but not contained by them.

Hermes is also the Psychopomp, the guide of the deceased to their destinations. It is significant that the Greeks considered such an utterly omnipresent and familiar God in daily life, the god of work and play and movement, to be the one who would accompany them out of it. It was surely a great comfort to them. Hermes is one of rather few Olympian gods for whom the underworld is open, and this chthonic aspect is also possibly part of why he's so closely associated with wealth in its mundane and mercantile forms rather than the more primal vitalistic sort of wealth symbolized by the germanic Fehu (ᚠ) rune and associated with gods like Indra.

Hermes is astrologically tied, of course, to the planet Mercury and thus to the two signs it rules, Gemini and Virgo. Gemini belongs to the element of Air and Virgo to Earth, which is fitting for Hermes as a traveller between planes. Gemini looks outward to form new connections between things, adapting itself easily to its objects, while Virgo seeks to perfect and organize everything under its purview. Together, they work to form and expand functional wholes.

Hermes' domain is as broad and varied as they come, and he is at work even in the things he doesn't specifically rule. You may have already seen that Hermes is extremely active in the modern world, seemingly to our detriment when we examine the empty, psychopathic chatter of liberal corporatism. Our societies have become inept at balancing and properly channeling Mercurial energies and our health has suffered in nearly every way imaginable. This is nothing to blame the God and shrink from him for, but all the more reason to engage him and to look for which parts of his teachings we may be neglecting.

A glaring example is his relationship with death. Our society has grown dangerously childish about death as we sequester an entire generation of our own elders into facilities where they face an absurd risk of abuse and neglect by strangers, not to mention widespread neurosis of a certain disease, the mishandling of which has certain provided precedent for similar failures in the future, possibly even involving much more dangerous pathogens.

This is all made possible by our own alienation from death, an alienation which is a disgraceful surrender to our most base instincts and which is enabled by the retreat of spiritual life from the public sphere. As like magnifies like, it is little wonder that a culture so unreceptive to Hermes' all-important work preparing us for death would be unable to receive him well in other ways.

The truth is that you are already dead and always dying. Your death has been written into the stars from the moment of your conception. Your death hangs from every word you speak and splashes like a puddle under every step you take. If you can hear this, and not just hear it but taste it, and understand what is asked of you, then you will know Hermes; always here, always helping, and always waiting to return you to the Absolute.

There is another, slightly less heavy lesson that we may be neglecting; our connections have become faster and faster and more and more voluminous as the internet ramps up, but have they become more *connective*? The epidemic of loneliness and psychosis suggests not. Hermes reminds us that we subsist not just in ourselves but in all the other emanations of the Supreme that we encounter, and that both ends of that line are equally important to Hermes' shepherding. Cultivating more respect for them, more intimacy even when that entails vulnerability, and more truth-telling even when that entails stubbed toes, is necessary. Moreover, it's an act of devotion, and devotion is the bridge between worlds.

To end on a more practical note, Hermes is especially helpful in endeavors of communication, exploration, commerce, and fitness - he is the patron not just of traders and teachers but also of gymnasia. It is often said that he appears in our lives as the orchestrator of small events and coincidences, often of a playful nature, so it is good to learn to spot these and give thanks for them.

Lord Hermes, swiftest and gentlest of all the Gods, friend of mankind, Evangelos, may you now come to our prayers, be pleased by our thanks, and carry our words to heaven to be heard by all the Gods.

Orphic Hymn 28 - Hermes

Hear me, Hermes, Maia's son,
Swift messenger of Zeus,
With an almighty heart, gentle guide of the dead,
Clever judge, Argeiphont

You of the coursing winged sandals
Are prophet and guide and friend to man,
Vigorous god, delighting in tricks,
Patron of all gymnasia,
Translator, all-speaker, profiting freely,
Wielding blameless tools of peace

Kyllenian lord, blessed and helpful,
Skillful in words and assisting good works,
A friend to every mortal in need,
Wielding that dreaded, most revered weapon,
The gentle tongue with noble mind.

May you come, blessed Hermes, attend to my prayer,
And grant a life of eloquence, of mindfulness and industry,
And when it ends, may you receive
My soul with peaceful clarity

Orphic Hymn 57 - Hermes Chthonios

All must tread the road which you keep, God,
Flowing but a single way,
Guiding souls through nether stillness.

Dionysian Hermes who revels in dances
With Venus' fluttering eyelids,
You haunt Persephone's sacred house
As guide to fateful souls
When they approach the destined harbor.

With your staff you grant them sleep,
And with your staff you wake them,
You who Kore trusts to lead
The everlasting souls of men

Blessed one, so dear to us,
May you grant us blessed ends
As you reward all labors

Hymn to Hermes Pankrates

Deceptive! How the beardless face and wiry limbs
Rush to weave
Shining circuits between firmaments
And all the fruitful heavens

Swift and kind, friend of man,
The vast divine
Strains to squeeze infinity
Into wand, and hand, and mind

Hermes' Prayer for Wealth

Kind lord Hermes, Laughing God,
Diplomat and merchant,
May you instruct our works and speech
And make them fruitful, if Lord Zeus wishes,
So that wealth may swell up high in your temples
And sweetly fill your suppliants' homes

Hermes' Friendship Prayer

Laughing Hermes, Prince of speech,
God of graceful thought,
May you send your charm and wit to lighten all my words,
Foster friendship with all I meet,
And tend my bonds with cheerful humor,
Thwarting petty squabbles with an honest tongue

Hermes' Mastery Prayer

Masterful Lord with quick, broad mind
Beloved Hermes, great and wise,
May you, unceasing, ever-present,
Kindly come to hear my prayer
And help perfect all of my works
With a swift genius and sharp tongue
That helps all men to teach and learn

Heimdall

Keeper of the Bridge of Light

Heimdall is a somewhat enigmatic God with three major pieces of information about him. Firstly, he is the watchman of Bifrost, granting or witholding passage into Asgard. Bifrost, the "Rainbow Bridge," is made of light and therefore can only be traversed by beings who are lighter than light. Ragnarok begins in earnest when Heimdall spots the fire giants approaching Bifrost and blows his horn to warn the gods. Secondly, Heimdall is said to have been born from nine etin sisters at the edge of the world. Some believe that these nine sisters were a mutated reference to the stars of the Pleiades cluster. If this is the case, then it would make Heimdall somewhat mythically cognate with both Hermes, the son of the Pleiad Maia, and Rudra, who was nursed by the "seven ladies."

The third bit of information, which deserves a more thorough treatment, is his appearance in the poem "Rigsthula," Where Heimdall travels to earth and goes about mankind disguised as the wandering "Rig," meaning "King." The poem is an account of Heimdall's gift of culture and rune-lore to mankind, as well as an attempt to explain the origin of the tripartite Indo-European caste system which is split between manual laborers, specialized workers, and a sacral warrior elite.

Rig first comes to a farmhouse where he beseeches the residents, Ai and Edda (meaning "great-grandfather" and "great-grandmother" for accomodations. They offer him the little food they have, and in return he gives them a son, named Thrall, who grows up strong but ugly. Rig then comes to the comely house of Afi and Amma, "grandfather" and "grandmother," who offer him a hearty meal and are reward-ed with a ruddy, handsome son, Karl. Finally Rig reaches the mansion of Fadir and Modir ("father" and "mother" of course) and is welcomed with a feast. Rig blesses this fam-ily with a beautiful and brilliant son, Jarl, who Heimdall takes under his wing and teaches the runes. When the boy is grown and educated Heimdall bestows on him the title Rig, and Jarl becomes mankind's first king.

While on its surface this narrative may seem unfair or fatalistic, especially to the first family, the sequential naming of the parents suggests that this may actually be a tale of one family's spiritual ascent throughought the generations via good works, culminating in kingship and the understanding of the world's secret foundations. Rig accords to mankind what is appropriate for their station, but also provides the path to betterment through righteous engagement with "ur-log," the karmic ur-law.

These families are also righteously interdependent; Thrall, the progenitor of laborers, provides the materials that Karl, the progenitor of craftsmen, makes useful and beauti-ful, and both castes are protected and given an aspirational direction by Jarl who is destined to himself become the Rig who makes the entire cycle possible.

These castes are also symbols of the tripartite soul which consists of Appetite, Will, and Reason; Appetite is concerned with physical immediacies, Will with the proper ordering of them towards useful ends, and Reason with exploring and understanding the origin and necessity of the whole system. Heimdall as the all-seeing watchman is especially emblematic of the inward-looking (rather than Apollonian upward-looking) Reason. Thus he permits passage over Bifrost only to the lighter-than-light, the unblemished, in other words those things which have become completely harmonious and self-united with their own divinity and therefore have no extraneous weight of Becoming hanging off of their full and radiant Being.

Heimdall is closely tied to Yggdrasil, being in a sense the world tree's sensory awareness of itself. This may also explain his nine mothers - the tree is made up of nine worlds. It is said that one of his ears sits at the roots of the tree, near Mimir's well. This association with Yggdrasil gives rise to his involvement with the Iwaz rune, ᛁ. Iwaz is the pillar of the world, the trunk of the world-tree, connecting the higher and lower in mutual generosity and containing the polarity between life and death, Helheim and Asgard.

The energetic wheels that occur along this axis, macrocosms of the same Hvels that swirl in the human being, are the light-bridges through which Heimdall sends his organizing and vivifying activities, with the completion of these activities being no less than the perception, understanding, and surpassing of them.

Heimdall is also tied to the rune Mannaz, ᛗ, which is the rune of mankind, his descendants. Mannaz is a mirrored Wunjo, ᛈ, as man is both a cause and experiencer of joy. Mannaz also contains Gebo, ᚷ, and Dagaz, ᛞ, both highly dualistic runes, connecting and balancing forces. Mannaz is the rune of sovereignty and the reflection that enables it. The proper use and purpose of spiritual sovereignty is to gain access to higher truths and to assist in their administration, sharing rather than avoiding the all-pervading and incomparably higher sovereignty of the Gods themselves.

Because he is the task-master and order-bringer, we look to him to help us bring the patterns of divine order into our own lives, and so he is of great importance to civil and family life. Come to him for increases in awareness and the exercise of your powers in accordance with that awareness.

Heimdall, Great Ancestor, may you now come to hear our prayers and behold our devotion.

Hymn to Heimdall

Upon the bridge of light you sit,
You all-beholding watchman,
With your eyes upon horizons
And your ear pressed to the Ash's roots
Father Heimdall, hail

You witness all our lives and days,
You hear our voices rise in prayer,
Eternal Seer, Eye of Heaven,
May you bring to Odin's chair
Our praises and our pleas

At ocean's edge, the edge of worlds,
Nine sisters bore one son,
A son of soil and frigid sea
With ram's blood burning tirelessly
Resounding and revealing

As Rig you came, Rig wise and strong,
To Edda and Amma and Moðir
And sons they bore, stout Thrall and Karl
And third the fair rune-winning Jarl
Who grew to gain your holy name

With kingly vision over all,
Establishing the laws of man,
You gave the plough and smithing-craft,
The fruits of peace in lawful lands
Where aesir are beloved

And when the times of trouble come,
When mischief frays the Ash's trunk
The golden God who wields the horn
Will sound, and all who hear will know
The trickster writhes beneath your boot

Heimdall's Prayer

All-beholding Heimdall, bringing order, Lord and Father,
May you grant me keenest vision,
May you join me to your works,
So that no speck of evil ever slips your golden fire

May you make my life abound
With light that works your glory,
And may you render laws most pleasing
To the needful sons of Man

Aphrodite

Venus, Kythereia

Aphrodite! She speaks for herself, though there is much to say about her that may surprise the reader. She is well-known and widely hailed as the goddess of love, a capacity in which even popular culture preserves her fame. Aphrodite is at work wherever there is desire and magnetism, which as it happens is nearly everywhere. She is active in families, friendships, communities, and most iconically in romantic bonds. She is responsible, however, not just for love between humans but also for the awe we feel for the gods and the caring providence that they supply for us. Her eros is the gravitational glue that holds the entire cosmos together.

Towards that end, her primary symbol is the mirror, though it is a slightly different mirror than that of Dionysus. What is symbolized by Aphrodite's mirror is the sympathy and similarity of the divine and its products, the seer and the seen. The reflection gazes back at her, and when she smiles, it smiles too. She is the goddess of what we may call, to borrow a term, Bhakti; intense, deeply personal, devotional worship, meant to unite oneself with a god.

Much has been written by spiritual masters about the necessity of overcoming desire and aversion in order to reach non-dual bliss and peace. It may therefore seem strange for the very goddess of desire and aversion herself to be so important for enlightenment, but in fact it is the awe and desire Aphrodite kindles in us that makes the unifying mission of worship possible in the first place. There is simply no other way to awaken the thirst for knowledge and piety in a person; they must learn that things they already desire, such as peace and happiness, will be attained through the gods. It is only later that you may convince them that the bond, the worship, is good in itself and for its own sake rather than just as an instrument for worldly life.

Related to this dynamic, we are told by the ancients of two different primary instantiations or darsanas of Aphrodite: Pandemos and Ourania. It was said that Ourania was primeval and hypercosmic, being born from the descent of Ouranos' castrated genitals into the sea. This is symbolic of the procession of the proliferating and generating principles of divinity into the waters of life which magnify and transmit whatever they absorb. Ourania was adopted by philosophers as the patroness of divine love, providence, and the pure joys of understanding and unification.

Aphrodite Pandemos, meaning "Aphrodite of all people", was said to be born from Zeus and Dione (Dione etymologically means "She-Zeus". It may refer literally to a female Zeus or else be a cognate for Hera from a different regional tradition or dialect). In this form the Goddess participates directly in wordly life as the irrepressible and unpredictable compulsion present in all creatures to love, connect, and breed. As source of this connection she is also naturally responsible for fear and hatred, since these things can only arise from desire and in response to obstacles against its fulfillment. With Pandemos, Ares proliferates bodies, while with Ourania Hephaistos proliferates forms and minds. In both cases Aphrodite does so because she is the beautifier and harmonizer, though her bond with Ares is stormy because the harmony of bodies is not fixed or guaranteed and requires dedicated effort both constructively and destructively to maintain.

Aphrodite is tied of course to the planet Venus and to its ruled signs of Libra and Taurus. These two signs could actually perhaps be tied, respectively, to Ourania and Pandemos. Libra surveys and balances, Taurus experiences and magnifies. Both of these signs are opposite the Mars-ruled signs of Aries and Scorpio, who balance them out: Aries supplies Libra with much-needed initiative and decisiveness, and Scorpio supplies Taurus with introspection, elaboration, and preparation. In turn Libra harnesses and subtly redirects Aries while Taurus soothes and secures Scorpio.

Academics consider worship of Aphrodite to most likely have been imported from the near eastern cult of Ishtar/Astarte, spreading into mainland Greece via Cyprus and Crete. While this is likely the case for large parts of her symbology and practice, She's by no means a "foreign" god in herself. Parts of her mythology suggest a connection to Eos, the goddess of dawn, which may have astrological origins with the planet Venus being seen at dawn and called the "morning star". It also cannot be ignored how congruent Aphrodite's functions are with those of Freya, as well as other goddesses. A Goddess of Love has simply been recognized in some form by most cultures, and the logical conclusions or mystic connections reached through that goddess seem to usually line up well with each other.

Venus is of great importance in Roman religion as an ancestor goddess. She was said to be the mother of Aeneas, the mythic founder of the Latin race, and was also claimed as an ancestor to the Julii clan to which Caesar belonged. Reportedly he himself greatly favored her in his own worship. There is even a rumor, though impossible to confirm, that the secret cultic name of the city of Rome/Roma, a stringently guarded secret epithet used in state rituals, may have been "Amor" - "Love".

When properly honored and heeded, Aphrodite turns arousal into a marriage whereby two people mutually reinforce and nurture each other. Ideally that love overflows, just as the One overflows, to create descendants who continue the ancestral cult and honor their forebears. When Aphrodite is spurned or ignored, arousal instead rears its head as a fruitless distraction that saps time and life force or even mutates into violence. When properly honored and heeded, Aphrodite makes hearty and healthful food sweet and brings us strength through it, while when spurned we may find ourselves guzzling empty food that leaves us drained.

As the goddess of desire we entreat Aphrodite to help us align our wants with what is right and virtuous, sublimating our urges into productive structures. This can apply to sex, food, money, power, and anything else that can become an object of desire. Aphrodite is a potent helper in these things, but she will want you to consider *why* you desire these things, what you wish to do with them, and how they may help or maybe even hinder your inner, spiritual life.

Divine Aphrodite, gentle Goddess, may you now come to hear our prayers, and may you grant that we will always desire what is most good.

Orphic Hymn 55 - Aphrodite

Ouranic Aphrodite, laughter-loving, widely sung,
Ocean born and granting births, nocturnal queen
And mother of Necessity, for everything proceeds from thee
Who caused the very cosmos to be drawn into its harmony;
You holy three-fold sovereign, origin of all which breeds
In heaven and on fruitful earth
And under Bacchus' raging sea.

You delight in feasts and weddings,
Happy mother of the Erotes,
Persuasive queen of secret joys,
Always here and always hidden,
The bright-tressed lovely heiress who arrives even unbidden,
You lupine, spousal friend of man
Whose scepter swirls with ribbon;

You bring us children, joy, and life,
And bond us to our fated pairs
As surely as you drive the frenzied beasts of land and sea,
So come, now, Cyprus' daughter, from wherever you may be
Whether on your incensed eastern throne
Or coursing through the wild steppe
Or flanked by your flock on the banks of the Nile
Or borne by swans across the waves

Delighted by youths as they dance in their circles,
Delighted by dark-eyed gaian nymphs
Delighted by dances on bright sandy beaches,
No place, great queen, escapes your reach
When maidens attend to your Cyprian seat;

They sing for you, Venus, and lovely Adonis
Just as we ourselves call out to you, happy Goddess
To draw us to harmony, to safeguard our sovereignty,
To furnish our lives with lovers and friends,
And to swell mortal hearts with piety

Proclus' Hymn to Venus

I sing of the many-named fountain of kings,
The foam-borne source of Erotes,
Of deathless, winged powers
Whose thoughtful bolts strike godly souls

To rouse our passions upwards
Towards their mother's fiery throne,
Or else to follow Zeus' lead
And fill the world with fruitful youth,
That marriage be the nearest thing
To earthly immortality,
Binding longing souls to birth
By Kythereia's will

O Goddess, hear, with ears that witness all,
Sprawled throughout the cosmos as its everlasting soul,
Or high in Aither far beyond the seven skies,
While pouring forth your powers
May you hear my humble prayer:

Mistress, steer me through life's troubles
And end, with righteous arrows,
The unholy sting of frigid lusts

Hymn To Aphrodite of the Waters

Where are you, Goddess? On the shores
Of rushing streams and roiling seas
The swirling foam calls out your name

From deep beneath you rise to seize
Our tongues, our eyes, our hearts,
Commanding mortals where you please
As deftly as the King of Heaven
Splits the blushing clouds

At edges of waters as surely as bedsides
We yearn to glimpse the laughing queen
Who beckons us from dripping throne

From deep below you rise to show
Your open heart, it pumps thick wine
Which courses in a steady flow
To gather us in worship
Of most holy Aphrodite

Aphrodite's Prayer

Peerless Aphrodite, beautiful divinity,
Gracefully you grant your charm to pleasant things
And forcefully you pull all mortals towards the Good.

May you match all people to their destined friends and pairs,
May you bring blissful comfort to the lonely and the seeking,
And may you help me, Goddess, to give and to receive
The boundless love that you enjoy
With a heart both strong and gentle.

Venus' Prayer for Piety

Lady Venus, Cyprian Queen, Ancestress,
As you guided the hearts of Aeneas and Caesar
So may you guide me, O Goddess.
You pull all souls into union,
Allotting their places and passions;
So may you fill my mortal heart
With inexhaustible awe, with reverence and love
And piety for all the deathless Gods.

Freya

The Warmaiden of Folkvangr

Freya is the goddess of love, war, magic, and prophecy, all for the same reason. She works the power of attraction through likeness, the power which enables all the mentioned activities. Romance can only exist when there is a love within both people that pulls itself towards its counterpart and war can only exist between two armed parties. Whenever the symmetry of these things is broken, their entire natures change. Unrequited love is mere obsession, uncontested war is mere slaughter. Magic, likewise, is simply the practice of manipulating physical imitations of non-physical things with the hopes of discovering or manipulating a corresponding non-physical motion. Sometimes, in turn, that motion is meant to have yet another echo in the physical world that produces a desired result.

Freya is the twin sister of Frey, the daughter of Njorth, and usually considered the wife of the otherwise poorly attested Odr. Most agree that this is just a kenning, splitting, or mutation of Odin. Likewise, there is debate over whether Freya and Frigge represent different instantiations of the same goddess, one being Asa and one Vanic.

It is said that Odr is endlessly wandering, and that Freya wanders in search of him. As she travels, she weeps for him and her tears turn to gold and amber. Perhaps this is meant to show that Freya is also a powerful transmuter of negative forces into positive ones, drawing out and distilling the good parts of bad circumstances. Certainly that is one of the functions of war, especially in the mind of the ancient Germanics. We are reminded of her position adjacent to Odin as a chooser of half of all battle-slain warriors; her portion goes to join her in the realm of Folkvangr, though sadly almost no other information survives about this belief. It is quite likely that these warriors are in roughly the same circumstances as those in Valhalla, passing their days feasting and training until being deployed to fight for the Aesir during Ragnarok. The overall function of this myth, of which cognates exist in several cultures, is to affirm for the warrior caste that their work is divinely sanctioned and that excelling in it is a valid form of religious pursuit.

As she drives attraction through likeness, Freya also illumines the reflections of ourselves that we see in other people and in our bonds to them. The revelations made by those bonds are of a similar nature to the revelations which are enabled by our bonds to the divine, as we witness ourselves in them just as the divine witnesses itself in the world. Ideally these revelations pull us closer to the people in our lives just as they pull us closer to the divine.

As a strongly magical goddess, Freya is involved in the entire rune row just as Odin is. She may be said, though, to have a special connection to several of the runes. Among these are Fehu, ᚠ, Algiz, ᛉ, and Ehwaz, ᛗ.

274

While Fehu's literal meaning is "Cattle," its meta-physical connotations are more Freyan in that it represents the attraction and then cyclical emission and re-attraction of wealth and power; cattle, in early pastoral society, were a mobile and fungible form of currency. Fehu is dynamic and present at all things' beginnings, and especially in the opening stages of young love, in order to call up the rest of the runic powers by their magnetic attraction to the force it projects and moves. When the rune row is arrayed in a circle to demonstrate its cyclical nature, Fehu comes immediately after the last rune of the row, Othala, which is the rune of heritage, property, and static, structured wealth. Othala is strongly Odinic, as much of Odin's attention is payed to defending the current form of the world against the reset of Ragnarok. Freya, meanwhile, is one of the survivors of Ragnarok and presides over the world's re-constituting.

Algiz, "Elk" or "Elk-sedge," is the rune of reaching towards the divine and accepting both the protection and the challenges that ensue. It is the rune of Valkyries, of discrimination between worthy and wanting. It is spiky, guarding what is within by keeping impurities out. These functions are only possible because of Freya's generous furnishing of our compulsion towards what is good and aversion to what is bad. Like Aphrodite, she wields these compulsions in service of their own overcoming, as well as channeling their productive energy to preserve the world while whosoever is able slowly makes their way towards her and towards the gods.

Finally, Ehwaz means "Horse." Its glyph, M, may be seen as two horses nuzzling each other. It is the rune of mutual trust and cooperation, the sort of bond necessary not just between horse and rider but between friends and lovers. Such a connection makes anything possible, even at astonishing speeds - the speed of luck or providence.

The rune is considered to be connected to the Indo-European mytheme of Divine Twins; the Ashvins, the Dioskouroi, Hengist and Horsa, Freya and Freyr, and possibly Apollo and Artemis. Wherever these twins appear they bring with them the mystery of dual-oneness, of being more than a sum of parts, and usually they are associated with travel and adventure. In the most worldly sense they celebrate a healthy mutual dependence that enables the participants to achieve much more than would be possible alone. In the most divine sense they represent the state of aligned flow that brings us to the divine and the divine into the world. Ehwaz can also be tied to the relationship between mind (rider) and body (horse), keeping this bond harmoniously ordered to both entities' benefit. The body or horse is a vehicle for the divine, and through Ehwaz we allow our friendships and parnerships to be vehicles for divine forces as well. It should be obvious how Freya factors into this, taking pride and joy in these connections and the ways they bring godliness into everyday life.

Freya, like Aphrodite, is eminently present and accessible and can be addressed for the same reasons. Honor her by being attentive in your relationships and watchful for the lessons they teach. Slow down and appreciate your surroundings, and give yourself time to experience yourself sprawling out into them to nourish and be nourished.

Holy Freya, may you come to hear our prayers and to reveal what is good.

Hymn to Freya

In banquets, beds, and battlefields,
Golden threads entwine
Lovers, friends, and foemen
All as cats before a mirror

Warlike Freya flits about
Here and there, you hold
Your sword in front of mortal eyes
Who gaze upon themselves;

To lovers you come forth as love,
To friends you come as friendship,
To those who love the din of war
You come with frightful carnage

And so to those who love the Gods
May you come forth as All,
Come forth with joy and holy fire
Through all the worlds Lord Ygg inspires

Freyasong

Freya is the gift of heaven,
Freya fills the sky-wide garth,
Freya's gift is dripping amber,
Freya fills the wisened heart

The blood of Cattle hotly flows,
The milk is Ymir's might,
The offering traverses worlds
In swirls of rose-gold light

The Antler spans the wings of swans,
The Valkuryar descend
To plant their feet in marshy soil
And gather chosen men

The Horse is loved by rider,
And the right hand washes left;
A wealth in kith and kindred
Is the wealth which gods love best

Freya is the gift of heaven,
Freya fills the sky-wide garth,
Freya's gift is dripping amber,
Freya fills the wisened heart

Freya's Friendship Prayer

Heavenly Freya, warlike, taking your allotted portion,
Patroness of warriors and all who share in hardships,
May you who strengthens mankinds' bonds
Safeguard our hard-won friendships

Athena

Minerva, Pallas Athene

Athena, the goddess of wisdom and heroism, serves as the ordering and enforcing principle of the physical world. Motion, Becoming, and chaos are properties of the sub-lunar, and Athena works to keep beings who are subject to these things as united as possible with their immortal, immutable divine cause. She is the great seamstress, weaving the network of connections and interactions that sustain the contingent world.

In a sense, she is the world's embodied mind. Thus while other gods are depicted naked or with light clothing, Athena and Ares are depicted with armor which represents embodiment and their engagement with the portions of embodiment which threaten to distract, erode, and profane the divine spark.

Athena is seen alongside heroes because the task of the classical hero is essentially spiritual. He aims to divinize himself through his works and through union with his cause. Athena comes swiftly to such people because at their summit such heroes are themselves performing the same work as she is: Executing and enforcing divine will and providence directly within the physical world.

Athena's act of divinizing and perfecting the world can be seen as a macrocosmic mirror of our own attempts to perfect ourselves. Just as Athena, in the course of her mission, comes to help people in their personal journeys, we must consider that the most perfect version of our own selves would likewise serve to guide and inspire others. It is good to remind ourselves that the pursuit of self-improvement is not actually selfish in the least, but is an act that tangibly strengthens the people and networks who rely on us.

There are many wonderful myths about Athena; the contest with Poseidon for patronage of Athens, her birth from Zeus' forehead, her many rescues of heroes and battles with giants, but the myth I will be treating on is one that is often poorly received by moderns: The metamorphosis of Arachne.

Arachne, a skilled weaver, believed she could weave a better tapestry than Athena. If taken symbolically, this is to say that Arachne believed she could create a better reality than a god could. This is the rallying cry of gnostics and atheists who look at the conflict and suffering that abounds in the world and choose to believe it exists out of malice, chance, or stupidity, rather than realizing that the dialectical motion of these things as they march to Athena's horn is actually the slowly grinding gears and long winding threads of a universe playing out the drama of divine beauty attempting to express itself in a space of limitation and separation.

Athena gave Arachne several chances to recant her hubris, but the girl persisted. When Athena challenged her directly to a weaving contest, Arachne created a work of flawless technical skill and precision, but she depicted scenes that cast the Gods as forces of predation and destruction, betraying an underlying lack of understanding. Arachne depicted ugliness extremely well; that doesn't create beauty. In punishment, she was turned into a spider, forever weaving sticky webs to trap small creatures in. We could say, rather than that it was a punishment, that Athena simply fulfilled the end result of the path Arachne had chosen, just as she fulfills the results of the paths heroes choose.

The human being who seeks to arrange material for its own sake rather than for any divine purpose is, in essence, insectoid. The larval soul is compelled to take the external-ities of material and ideology and weave a cocoon for itself. Some cocoons may be prettier or more effective than oth-ers, but they are useless if they are never left behind by the emerging butterfly.

Today, without rites of passage and adequate mytho-poesis, there is an epidemic of larvae who dote over their cocoons of identities and pet ideologies, comparing them with those of others in a contest of ego and status. Luckily many feel in their souls that something is lacking from this equation; yet when going in search of that piece, just by the nature of how the mind works, they are forced to filter things through the lens of their cocoon. This is normal and nat-ural, but contact with truth, with reality at its most primal and immanent, should slowly erode the cocoon rather than reinforce it. Athena is the bridge between the cocoon and the butterfly, beginning our journeys with physical impulses and slowly building an edifice up which we may climb.

When you refuse to allow that erosion and construction to happen, when you reject the fullness of experience and understanding provided by the Gods and mediated through the traditional symbology we have co-created with them, you are committing the hubris of Arachne.

I can guarantee that most of what you consider good and true right now is discursive. It might not be "wrong," but it's probably occupying way too much mental space and importance. You may cling to these things because they are all you know, but in this you are like an apple stubbornly refusing to drop from the branch even as December approaches. Just as Arachne was punished by being allowed to let her own hubris consume and transform her, the rejection of philosophy, virtue, and devotion in favor of preserving the cocoon will leave you larval forever.

If you are going to build what is truly good, what is truly fulfilling, what is truly human, the tangled garment of impulses, distraction, desires, and contingencies is not going to do you any good. You are going to have to face reality in its most primal, terrifying, transcendent form and bring yourself to acknowledges its goodness. This is what Athena, spear in hand, does eternally, and what she takes us under her wing to learn.

It is only once this contact is reestablished, false attachments released, and genuine awe and reverence for raw Being in all its forms internalized, that a tapestry of proper structure and relations can be woven according to the correct priorities. What you actually want is probably not what you think you want. Humble yourself and let Athena guide you to your goals.

Address the goddess for help in any craft or discipline, as well as for matters of learning and practice. She may also help you to get in a good flow when working or moving, as the flow state is a state of mind-body unity. Athena is highly protective, and you may find her sometimes at moments of risk or high-stakes decisions. She is tasked with protecting us from ourselves just as much as from the world, and is best received when we get in touch with our highest selves.

Divine Athena, Tritogeneia, Polymetis, may you now come to hear our prayers and guide our hands.

Orphic Hymn 32 - Athene

Wide-sung Pallas, sole begotten, Zeus' happy warlike child,
Rushing forth from heaven's mind, invincible Athene,
Brave in battle's shrieking din,
Ineffable, yet friend to man

You sprint the wind-swept hills and peaks
And tower over gentle vales
Delighting in arms and landscapes both

Athletic maiden, gorgon-slayer, hot tempered mother of arts,
You shun the bed where lovers lay
And mete out madness to the blind
Yet bless the strong with wisdom

Impetuous one, shrewd androgyne,
Polymorphous dragoness,
Muse and reverend, great revealer,
Equestrian killer of giants

Tritogene, victorious, deliverer-from-sorrows,
By day and even darkest night
May you hear our prayers, O bright-eyed Queen,
And prosper our seasons with boundless health.

Proclus' Hymn to Athena

Hearken, child of the Father, Born of Aegis-bearing Zeus,
Springing forth from Jovian source atop your mighty series,
With manly heart, exceeding strength,
You brandish that most holy shield

Tritogene, great Pallas, wielding lances and a golden helm,
Hearken to this hymn, Athena, with a most kind heart
And suffer not my words to scatter in the ruthless winds

You who threw the gates of wisdom open,
Gates where Gods have trod,
You who threw the giants down and slew them
When they took up arms,
You who held your girdle tightly steadfast
Against Vulcan's lust

You who saved the untouched heart of Bacchus
When the titans rent his infant limbs,
For Zeus had willed that Dionysos
Once again sprout up to life

With your axe, Athena, you sever at the neck the heads
Of Hekate's passion-demons as they try to drag us down;
You, Athena, put to rest the process of becoming,
You whose power wakens mortals by the love of virtue

You adorn our life with skill in all of our endeavors,
You forge the very faculty of craft within our souls,
You, who won your temple on the highest-crested hill,
And made of it a symbol of your series-leading work

You who loves the land whose bounty feeds the noble man,
You who loves the letter and the books that nourish minds,
You who thwarted Neptune's will
And staunched his grand desire
To possess that noble city where you made the Olive sprout,
A sign of your great victory against the raging, roaring sea
When gulfs and waves rose up to lash the land

Hearken, you whose holy face must flash with fierce light,
And grant my soul a blessed harbor as it roams the earth;
Let your love & wisdom shine a beacon through your myths

Breathe into my heart a love with such exceeding might
That it drags me from the vaults of matter
Back to high Olympus where great Jove makes his abode

And if I ever fall in error, set upon by profane acts,
Offenses which all men commit with our most foolish spirit,
Then may you, great Athena, most gracious in your counsel,
Preserve me from the wrath of furies,
For you are mankind's warden, and I am yours to keep

May you provide my limbs with steady and most holy health,
And drive away the bitter wasteful hordes of hungry illness;
I beg you, Basileia, to halt the course of misery
With your most holy hand

Send your calm winds to my voyage;
Send a spouse and children, fame and joy,
Persuasion, wit, and power, with high honors among men,
And victory against all foes;

Hearken, Goddess, to these words, the words of the devoted,
I ask you with most needful heart to lend a gentle ear

Hymn to Minerva

Great Minerva, stout and kind,
We call you from your father's side
To come bearing Victory, Justice and Peace,
And weave for us heroic robes

Holy Minerva, come bearing the aegis,
Wrapped in the glory of your noble purpose,
Come teach us the precepts of Law, Skill, and Honor,
So that Jove may pour out for us Life, Wealth, and Valor

For blind is the eye which lacks you, great maiden,
Blind is the land without craft, tact, and grace,
And you are the anchor of signs, tools, and language,
By whom we may know all the Gods' blessed names

Protector, defender, preserver, Minerva,
With righteous and masterful mind may you come
To sharpen our bodies and build up our temples,
And to make all our offerings clean, fat, and strong

Hymn to Athena

Erupting forth from Zeus' brow,
Warlike maiden, spanning skies
And smiling when we call to you
From gentle fields or churning seas

Tutor of stout Herakles,
Guide of lost Odysseus,
Standing near to lift us up
When we choose the hero's path

May you, much-loved Athena,
Come to teach and hone and raise us
So that our works approach perfection
Mirroring the deathless Gods

Athene's Prayer for Virtue

Aegis-Bearing Athene, beloved daughter of Zeus,
You who lights bright fires on the brows and heads of heroes,
May you ignite my heart and limbs
With thirst for godly virtue,
And the strength to rightly think, speak, act, and live

Ares

Mars, Enyalios

Ares, known to the Romans as Mars, is the God of Warfare. As moderns for whom actual war has grown distant, it's easy for us to neglect him. The "warfare" of this god, though, can be any conflict no matter how small. In daily life nowadays this very often means conflict with ourselves; getting out of bed, going to the gym, things that your body might drag its feet about. Lifting weights is also called "resistance training". Mars does this on a cosmic scale, sharpening things through their opposition to each other.

He is the lover of Venus, goddess of beauty and connection, because warfare is simply a manner of relationship, one which can perfect and beautify what it doesn't destroy. Of course, in order for Mars to beautify through opposition, it is necessary for things to be split in the first place. To illustrate this, Mars is considered one of the few direct sons of Juno, the mother of multiplicity who translates Jupiter's being into plural beings. Mars then echoes his mother's function further down the chain of causation by translating Athena's causal paradigm of united, ordered Body into the multitude of bodies in the world.

You may also notice that Mars and Ares have quite different "tones" to their cultus and mythos - this is a matter of different emphases, with the Greeks having a theophany that emphasizes the oppositional chaos of war while the Romans saw war as a disciplined and cooperative endeavor that strengthened their state and paradoxically preserved its internal peace.

Mars, of course, presides over the planet Mars, which rules aggression and how we approach conflict. He and his planet are the rulers of the signs of Aries and Scorpio. These two signs can be seen, respectively, as Martial force being projected outward by Aries or turned inwards by Scorpio.

Aries is the first sign of the zodiacal calendar (similarly, March was the first month of the pre-julian Roman calendar) and rules over beginnings, overflowing energy to an almost chaotic degree, and impulsive Will. Scorpio meanwhile resides in the height of autumn when things prepare for their seasonal death. Scorpio exists in that space in order to remind us that the preparation for death is the preparation for rebirth, and with its claws it digs through our attachments and severs the ones that are not fit to survive the winter. Aries is action, Scorpio is reaction. Aries is initiation, Scorpio is intimacy.

Mars' trials clear away rotting wood and dead weight and allow us to break through entropy by inducing spiritual hormesis, introducing enough trouble to trigger an opposite response that leaves us better off than before. Times when Mars' influence is strong are great opportunities to start new things, as we have just that little extra kick to actually turn ideas into reality.

Ares is present whenever you are faced with any sort of challenge. Mars is tough love, getting up in our faces and spitting on our comfort. This culture will remain alienated from his gifts of life-bringing fire, adventure, victory, and understanding until it remembers how to embrace struggle with equanimity and faith.

Conflict is as much an invitation to rise above it and see it from an eagle-eye view as it is a question of victory. To this end, honor Ares' sparring partner Athena by studying as hard as you fight. Their mythical opposition is symbolic of cooperation. As children of Zeus, they are vital parts of the journey back towards the highest reality which he curates and mediates.

To honor and connect with Mars, be tough on yourself in constructive ways. That doesn't by any means include self-flagellating or fixating on poor self-esteem. Such defeatism is disrespectful to the God who works so forcefully to bring us good things. You must remember the fundamental symmetry, congruence, and shared origin of your self with its source, and allow the great destroyer to sever the seat of your consciousness from the tangled mass of worldly troubles as you learn to become the seer and not the seen. There is no point to fear. Fate is fated; you will die. Just go to war and trust the Gods. Arjuna found Krishna on a battlefield.

Father Mars, may you come to hear our prayers, to drive and inspire us, to preserve what is righteous, and dispose of what is not.

Orphic Hymn 65 - Ares

Unbreakable, strong-hearted, valiant God,
Man-slaying stormer of walls, joyed by arms,
Armor-rattling Ares, flecked with gore,
Rejoicing in clamor, in horrors of war

Lusting for the clash of spears,
Obscene and museless carnage,
Halt your raving strife, O God,
And cease to grieve our pain-gripped hearts

Yield to Bakkhos and Cyprian Venus,
Yield your might to Demeter,
And grant us strength to uphold peace,
A peace to nourish bliss and youth

Hymn To Civic Mars

To you, great Mars, O forceful one,
Who girds the waist of blooming youth
I sing, I sing and strike and roar
With fervent praise, with thankful praise

Mars enthroned in red and from the root discharging
Vigor to climb the coiled spine
And straighten like spears all crooked things

Mars enthroned in red and from Your seat discharging
War to cauter open wounds and War to cleanse
The rot which gathers on still waters

For Yours is the fire, O fiery King
Which burns in tight stomachs and pulses in limbs,
Which strikes forth in tongues to win riches and fame

And Yours is the spark, O striking God,
The spark to light up Vesta's hearth where Venus' linens lay
Just as Yours are the walls, O steadfast Lord,
The brazen, fleshy walls of Men

Hymn to Adventuring Mars

Wherefore! Wherefore does vicious clap of oar
Resound piously 'gainst rock and wave?
Wine-dark sea's too-soft flesh heaves
To and fro, teasing and jostling
The rapid, breathy face of War

Herefore! Herefore does Mars drive lofty sword
'Cross wide-chested Ocean with abundant lungs:
That Ice and Rime shall be demise
Of un-exultant voice and of
Lustless limbs, paltry in force

Herefore! Sun and Bronze alike on kindred arms
Bear down zealously with glistening violence
That smitten thigh in shame may drive
Man forth from shady womb
By just decree of baleful Mars

Hymn to Victorious Ares

Ares, Striking God, spear-wielder,
Frenzied vanguard of the seasons,
May you with limbs and heart which swell
With coursing blood and fire
Take us underneath your wing to learn the ways of power,
Teach us to begin our works with dogged feline minds
And trample down all obstacles as Bacchus treads the vine

We dedicate our works to you, we dedicate our spoils,
And thank you for our victories
Whenever blessed Zeus decrees
That boots and blood and hardtack take us far from home

Ares' Prayer for Strength

Lord Ares, striker, beginner, vanguard,
May you, giver of life and force,
Fill my mind and body with strength
So that my trials all bear fruit
And bring me towards perfection

Mars' Pacification Prayer

Prosperous Mars, abundant in forceful life,
Lord of the fields and the fences which keep them,
Protector of the towering wall,
May you guide us in war and in peace
And remind us to cherish those restful days
That only strenuous effort can win

Tyr

The War-Judge

Tyr is the god of war in a very particular way. Tyr is the separator of heaven and earth and the selfless enforcer of natural law. Tyr asks "what is Right?" and carries it out at any cost. Thus he grants victory to the side of any conflict that built up the better urlog - the side whose karma is most perfectly aligned with the universal karma. He is able to do this because as a god he himself transcends karma, applying it to the things below him in such a way as to make the same transcendence possible for us. Tyr forces us to forgo greed and fear in all our pursuits, asking that we act without the childish sense of entitlement to our labors' fruits. This is because what is most right is to realize that the labor and its results are mere motion and Becoming, unworthy of attachment.

What is worthy of attachment and devotion is not the result of Becoming, but rather its origin, because Becoming is by definition the incomplete or temporally divided imitation of Being. That said, there are of course forms and ways of Becoming that are more complete, more divine, than others, and Tyr is the guardian of that distinction and the dispenser of these ways to those who have earned them according to their own actions.

Tyr was invoked both in war and in criminal trials for the same reason: For the ancients, to invoke justice in all things, even if it invites judgement of oneself, was most pious, and piety is the work which brings about the way-of-Becoming from which one can most easily honor, adore, and join the Absolute.

Tyr is best known for the sacrifice of his hand to the wolf-etin Fenrir. Fenrir, representative of destructive (rather than primordial) chaos and disorder, was brought into Asgard as a puppy but grew so large so quickly that the gods grew alarmed. They began attempting to bind him with various ropes and chains, playing it off to Fenrir as a friendly challenge to test his strength. The wolf broke bond after bond and continued accepting the challenges out of pride. Eventually the gods grew desperate and approached the master dwarven craftsmen, asking them to forge an unbreakable net. The dwarves did so by using impossible materials like "the breath of a fish" or "the sound of a cat's footsteps", and the resulting net, Gleipnir, was extremely subtle and nearly invisible. Fenrir was suspicious of it because of its apparent weakness, so he would only accept the challenge to break free from it if one of the gods would place their hand in his mouth as insurance. Only Tyr stepped forth, and when Fenrir realized he could not escape from this binding he bit down and severed the god's hand.

Symbolically, this is to say that Tyr sacrifices his wholeness, part of his power and sovereignty, in order to ensure that there is still divine involvement in the lower world which is wracked by chaos. As painful as it is, he allows his hand to be severed both so that creation is not lacking creative power and so that creation remains distant enough from that power that it maintains its cold, wet, contingent existence. The alternative is for it to be swallowed entirely by the growing wolf of entropy; Tyr upholds the distance of this world between both fire and ice because it has been deemed just by the Gods that this place should exist as a battleground and a courtroom.

Tyr's rune is the eponymous Tiwaz, ↑, the rune of justice and sacrifice and of the victory that results when they are present. It pictographically depicts both a spear-head and the vault of heaven being upheld by the world-axis which separates and therefore maintains heaven and earth. It can also be thought of as pointing north towards the pole-star, which was associated with Tyr because of its unchanging position. Certainly something which helps men to navigate in unknown territory is a good symbol of the God who says "These are the laws, and these are their results; victory, death, or both."

Address Tyr in times of decision and temptation when you are called upon to make uncomfortable sacrifices. He is the power of equal and opposite reaction; good and bad deeds have their just rewards, even if our human minds are unable to distinguish them from each other at times. His work can also be slowly cumulative as your actions compound on each other, and perhaps finally bear fruit when you are most in need.

Lord Tyr, may you now hear our prayers, receive them kindly, and welcome purifying justice into our lives.

Hymn to Oathkeeping Tyr

Vicious teeth in rotting gums
Arrayed in crooked rows,
You stained your godly hand
Amidst the waves of spit and bile,
You held your vow as sacred,
And those jaws upheld their own

Not a tear escaped your eye,
Your all-beholding, judging eye,
As fenris-wolf laid rightful claim
To that which Odin promised,
For you, our fearless father,
Know so well the price of War

Father Tyr, uphold for us the oaths we swear by you,
And make us fierce and fearless
When our promises come due
So that the squirming tides of War
Will not erode our honor

Tyr's Prayer

Father Tyr, staunch and vast, upholder of the world,
Meting out your justice by the sword,
May you harden like fired steel
My stomach, limbs, and heart
So that they may withstand good deeds
When honor asks for sacrifice

Hestia

Vesta

Hestia is the goddess of the hearth and its fire. She is addressed at the beginning and end of all offerings, as she was the first child of Kronos to be born and swallowed as well as the last child to be disgorged. In Plato's *Cratylus*, Socrates suggests that her name derives from "ousia," meaning "essence" or "being." She is associated by later platonists with matter: It is said that matter, as a formless and perfectly passive thing which is given form from above, is both an immediate result of the Supreme Principle and the border between its being and its non-being. It is understandable for this position to be taken as symbolic of Being, because within this world our sense-organs percieve being through the lens of the material.

Hestia is vital to religious life because her fire burns away the chilly "anti-matter" that holds things in their physical form, revealing the energetic nature of reality. Our sympathetic beholding of her fire and the transfer of offerings through it brings about that same revelation within ourselves. This is not to say of course that matter is bad or totally undesirable, only that what is best in it and most desirable within it is the portion of it that is fiery rather than frozen, relaxed rather than tensed, upwards-reaching rather than downwards-falling. Hestia encourages us to cultivate attention to this portion by preserving her fires in the home and in the polity.

Hestia is the priestly counterpart to Hermes. While Hermes travels, Hestia maintains a continuous and rooted presence, ideally in flames that are never extinguished such as those of the Roman temple of Vesta. Hermes connects the disparate while Hestia denies disparity altogether. Combined these two gods attest to the law of the conservation of energy, that nothing is created or destroyed (Hestia) but only transmitted or transformed (Hermes). No matter where one goes or what form one inhabits, Hestia will be there in the exact same way as she always is; even in Olympus she tends the hearth of the Gods.

Hestia does not really participate in any mythic drama. There are only two important narratives directly involving her: First, the already discussed swallowing and disgorgement by Kronos. Secondly, it was said that Apollo and Poseidon, Intellect and Being, desired her hand in marriage. Hestia desired to remain unwed, and Zeus granted her wish. He appointed her the maiden of the hearth and the center of all homes.

She is an unwed, childless virgin because she does not produce any further unfolding of particulars from herself in the way that Poseidon and Apollo do, and she is the center of homes because that consistency and unchangeability gives the family the space in which they themselves may "unfold" and evolve throughout their generations.

The Hearth is the centerpiece of the home, as it is where meals are cooked and shared. Every such meal was thought of by the ancients as a sacrament of union between all the members of the familias, renewing its continuity and connection every day. This importance to the family as their grounding and as their link to each other and to the divine is extrapolated and scaled up to the political scale as well, as every town ought to have its own hearth at its center in order to sanctify itself as an extended family-of-families. This was the function of Rome's Vestal Virgins, chaste priestesses who tended Vesta's sacred fire. These priestesses were active, important, and powerful political figures, and their opinions carried weight in the senate as well as in criminal proceedings. To speak idiomatically, it was almost as if the entire city of Rome had institutionalized the position of that aunt who is always organizing extended family get-togethers and mediating their drama.

In our own lives, Hestia should be called upon for presence, coherence, and spiritual hygeine in everyday life and especially in the home. She *is* the metaphysical subsistence of the home, one of the most important and foundational things in our lives, and should be extensively and deeply appreciated for this.

Kind Hestia, may you now hear our prayers, and may you bring them by your fire to the ears of all the Gods.

Orphic Hymn 84 - Hestia

Holy Hestia, Kronide daughter,
Mistress of the endless fire,
Dwelling in centers, in hearths and in heaven,
May you purify your suppliants

Please grant us wealth and holiness,
Benignant minds with youth unending,
You, our anchor, heaven's buttress,
Dwelling place of deathless Gods

Eternal, vibrant, much-beloved,
Happy one with many forms,
May you receive this offering
And breathe upon us soothing health

Hymn to Purifying Vesta

Holy Vesta, Thousand-throned
Yet always at the center,
May you who rules the blazing hearth
Rise up to warm our weary souls,
And rise to burn us clean

Great Goddess, rise to hear our words,
And come accept our gifts,
Maiden Vesta, ever-present,
Bear witness that we thank you

Hymn to Cosmic Vesta

You are shining stillness -
At every altar to the Gods
Your flickering hands rise
And grip us in your unceasing prayer.

Kind silence, O Goddess,
Is the fire coiled in your lap;
Sleeping cats stretch
To the farthest star

Vesta's Prayer for Purification

Holy Vesta, great goddess,
Maiden master of the hearth,
May you burn away miasma
So that we may approach the Gods
With clean hands, minds, eyes, and hearts

Vesta's Household Prayer

Eldest Vesta, holy one, beloved maiden of the hearth,
Warm and nurturing center of homes,
You are the quiet axis of our house.

May you welcome us into your presence,
May you call our ancestors to join,
And may you bless and drive all of our duties
And our bonds as parents and heirs.

Fin.

*May all the Gods bless you and
preserve you in your travels*

Made in United States
Orlando, FL
12 March 2022

15678216R00193